THE WORLD AWAKES

THE WORLD AWAKES
THE RENAISSANCE IN WESTERN EUROPE

Polly Schoyer Brooks
and
Nancy Zinsser Walworth

J. B. LIPPINCOTT COMPANY
Philadelphia · New York

Library of Congress Catalog Card Number 62-17234

Printed in the United States of America

First Edition

ACKNOWLEDGEMENTS

We wish to thank our husbands, Ernest Brooks, Jr., and Edward H. Walworth, Jr. for their helpful criticism throughout the writing of this book. We also want to thank our friend, Walter Lord, for suggesting the title.

We are grateful to the New Canaan Public Schools for inspiring us to write the book, to the New York Public Library for its kind assistance and to the Art Reference Bureau of Ancram, N.Y., for its Alinari and Anderson photos.

CONTENTS

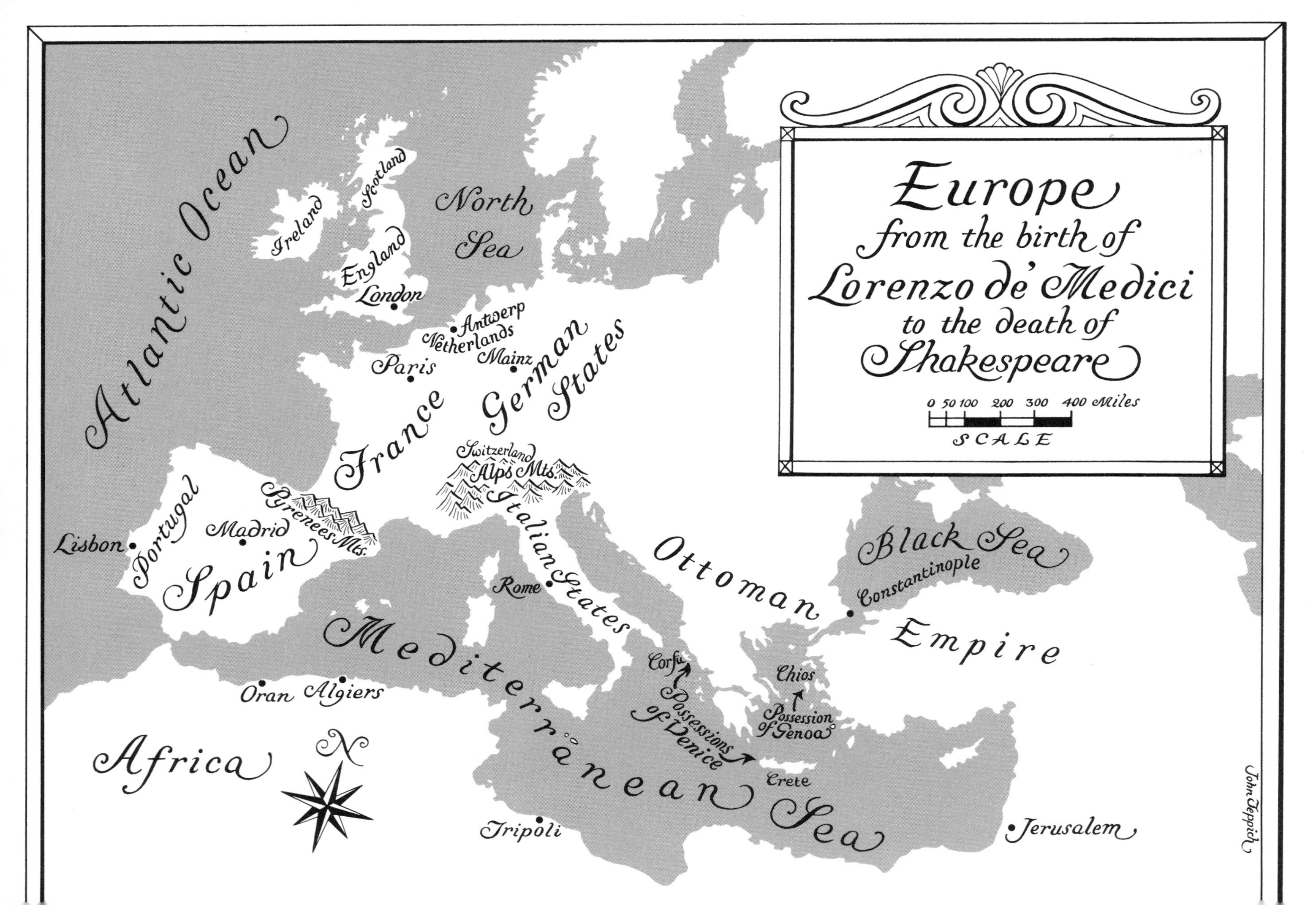
Europe
from the birth of
Lorenzo de' Medici
to the death of
Shakespeare
0 50 100 200 300 400 Miles
SCALE
Atlantic Ocean
Ireland
Scotland
England
London
North Sea
Antwerp
Netherlands
Paris
Mainz
France
German States
Switzerland
Alps Mts.
Italian States
Portugal
Lisbon
Madrid
Spain
Pyrenees Mts.
Rome
Ottoman Empire
Black Sea
Constantinople
Corfu
Possessions of Venice
Chios
Possession of Genoa
Crete
Mediterranean Sea
Oran
Algiers
Africa
N
Tripoli
Jerusalem
John Teppich

THE WORLD AWAKES

Mont St. Michel, a medieval abbey-church, rises from an island off the northeastern coast of France.

FRENCH GOVERNMENT TOURIST OFFICE

FROM the cold North Sea to the warm Mediterranean a new era was dawning. The Western world was waking up.

Since the barbarian invasions and the fall of Rome in A.D. 476, Europe had been asleep. The great Greek and Roman civilizations were buried as the Dark Ages descended on the Western world. But after a few centuries of darkness the barbarian tribes settled down into a feudal way of life and the Middle Ages began.

During the Middle Ages the Christian Church was the most powerful influence in Europe. The great crusades with their armored knights and daring exploits were carried out for the sake of Christianity. Men built lofty cathedrals, rising toward heaven, for the glory of God. Plays depicted heaven and hell right on the stage. People were more concerned with afterlife than with life on this earth. They prepared their souls for heaven and feared hell.

In those medieval days life was violent and lawless. Feudal lords spent their time raiding other lords. Each noble with his castle, and his knights and peasants paying homage to him, was a law unto himself. He was like a king in a little kingdom. Nobles, ladies, and knights lived in huge fortified castles. Peasants, bound to the land like slaves, lived in huts. They had little human dignity or feeling of being individuals.

But life is always changing. Feudalism was to die out, towns to grow, and nations to emerge. New forces and ideas were struggling to break the confines of the medieval world. A wonderful new era, the Renaissance, was beginning.

Various things brought about these changes. In the fourteenth century a horrible plague, known as the Black Death, swept over Europe. People died by the thousands. So many peasants died that there were not enough left to till the soil for their lords. This dreadful calamity was a help to the peasants who were left. They were now so much in demand that they were offered money instead of just a plot of land. Some moved on to nobles who offered higher pay. Some earned enough money to buy their freedom and moved to towns.

With this shortage of labor the nobles had a hard time keeping up their castle life, and when guns and cannon were perfected, castles lost their importance as strongholds. For even the thickest castle wall could not withstand the attack of cannon. Knights encased in heavy armor had been protected against the thrust of a spear or the blow of a mace. Against bullets and cannon balls they were defenseless. Knights and castles became unimportant. Nobles began to lose their power. They lowered their drawbridges more frequently. Some even cut large windows in the walls to let in the light. Castles became less gloomy and castle life less fearsome.

Attack on a castle in late medieval times. Note the few new cannon as well as the medieval weapons of long bow, cross bow and lance.

PIERPONT MORGAN LIBRARY

The interest in life shifted to the towns. Towns were the center of trade and craftsmanship. The peasants who flocked to the towns joined craft guilds, organized to protect the workers. There were all kinds: stonecutters, weavers, bakers, goldsmiths, and merchants. Some of these guilds later developed into the famous Renaissance workshops where such great individuals as Leonardo da Vinci first learned their trades.

Trade was expanding rapidly. Spices, dyes, jewels, and alum

from the East, fish from the North Sea, wool from Spain and England were traded along the Mediterranean seaports or inland over the winding passes of the Alps. Trade helped the growth of towns and trade created wealth. As trade increased some of the more ambitious merchants went beyond the limits of the guilds. Their enterprises were far-flung. For instance, a wool merchant might add to his enterprise the importing of dyes and alum, needed in the making of cloth. He could then control the whole process of cloth manufacture. These merchants were the forerunners of modern capitalists.

With the increase of trade, money became important. In feudal days trade had been simple exchange of goods, but as trade increased merchants needed money for their business. Goldsmiths who made coins as well as jewelry became bankers. They often kept money in their vaults for merchant friends. When they had a surplus they would lend money at interest. The famous Medici bankers started as goldsmiths.

These merchants and bankers were creating a new class of townspeople—a moneyed class. The feudal lord's wealth had been wealth of land and vassals. This new merchant wealth was based on money, earned by clever and ambitious men. With this wealth came leisure and a desire for the refinements of life. Some of these wealthy merchants and bankers became great patrons of art and learning.

As the power of the nobles declined, the power of kings rose. Kings looked to the towns for wealth and support. Townspeople began to count on their kings for protection against lawless nobles. With town wealth a king could have a government of law and order. The townspeople saw the advantage of supporting a king, for under his protection they could pursue their interests in peace. Soon one king and one court controlled one nation, and powerful monarchs such as Ferdinand of Spain, Francis I of France, and Elizabeth I of England entered the game of politics and balance of power.

The great Christian Church was changing too. It was becoming wealthy and the papal court at Rome was more splendid than a king's. The Popes of the Renaissance became patrons of art and

Colleoni, a famous Italian mercenary of the late 15th century, by Verrocchio.

BETTMAN ARCHIVES

learning as well as spiritual leaders of the Christian world. They too were drawn into politics as kings became more powerful and menaced the papal authority. Monarchs resented the power and wealth of the Popes. They wanted the church money, which flowed annually to Rome, for themselves and their own countries.

Professional soldiers now took the place of medieval knights. These soldiers, called "mercenaries," were willing to fight for anyone who hired and paid them well. The mercenaries sometimes formed free companies, fighting first for one side, then the other. These professional soldiers were often skilled but not always reliable. They were usually more interested in their pay than in the cause for which they fought. National, permanent armies developed gradually, but methods of warfare changed rapidly with the increased use of guns and cannon.

Setting type in an early print shop.

In the fifteenth century a wonderful invention opened up new fields of interest and learning. In the little German town of Mainz, John Gutenberg invented the first printing press with movable type. This meant that many books could be printed quickly. In the Middle Ages only the monks and a few scholars had been able to read and write, for books, beautifully and laboriously written by hand, had been rare. They had been kept in monasteries, not available to the people. But the invention of printing shed a new light on the world. The Bible and other books were printed and the world began to read.

In the search for easier routes to the wealth of the Orient, vast continents were discovered. In the Middle Ages men had not ventured very far into the dreaded Sea of Darkness, the Atlantic

Ocean. They had been afraid they would fall off the edge of the world. But the interest in trade and the desire for wealth opened the door to the great age of discovery. In 1492, Columbus discovered America. Proof that the world was round was established. Merchant ships plied the oceans of the world, bringing wealth and trade to the Atlantic seacoast of Europe.

All these changes—the growth of towns, nations, and wealth, the use of gunpowder and printing, and the expansion beyond the seas—helped bring about the end of the Middle Ages and the beginning of a new era, the Renaissance.

The word "Renaissance" literally means rebirth. It was first used to describe a new interest in the ancient classics—the great writings and works of art of the wonderful Golden Ages of Greece and Rome. The writings of the old philosophers, the sculpture and architecture of the ancient masters—all filled the Renaissance world with awe and delight.

But the Renaissance means much more to us than a rebirth of interest in the glories of ancient Greek and Roman civilizations. It means a way of life which started in Italy and passed beyond the Alps to France, Spain, and England. It was a glorious awakening from the narrow confines of a feudal world to the joyous discovery of a wider, freer world.

In the Middle Ages men had banded together in a joint effort to praise God. During the Renaissance man as an individual became important. His effort to perfect himself in all things has given us the term "Renaissance man," a man of many interests and accomplishments.

Driven by their intense interest in a newly discovered world, and aided by the leisure which the new wealth provided, the great individuals of the Renaissance developed ideas, art, and a culture that are our inheritance; on them we have built our modern world.

N
Duchy of Milan
Milan
Republic of Venice
Venice
Po River
Genoa
Florence
Arno R.
Republic of Florence
Papal States
Rome
Adriatic Sea
Corsica
Sardinia
Mediterranean Sea
Kingdom of Naples
Naples
Kingdom of Sicily
The Italian States
in the time of
Lorenzo de' Medici
and
Leonardo da Vinci
0 50 100 150 Miles
SCALE

PART 1
ITALY AWAKES

The hill town of Vinci, near Florence. Birthplace of Leonardo.

ITALIAN STATE TOURIST OFFICE

THE long narrow country of Italy reaches from the snow-capped Alps in the north to hot, dry Sicily in the south, almost cutting the Mediterranean Sea in two. Its coast line is over twenty-five hundred miles long, and few areas in the entire country are more than fifty miles from the sea. A chain of mountains sweeps down much of its length, occasionally interrupted by broad green river valleys. On many of its hills stand the ruins of ancient Roman villas and medieval castles. Poets have celebrated Italy's lovely countryside from the earliest days, praising its mountain streams and vineyards and the flowers that shine in the bright Italian sun.

Throughout history the merchant with his goods and the invader with his sword have been tempted by Italy's long coast line. Phoenicians, Greeks, Moors, and Normans were among the many people who settled and flourished in Italy at one time or another.

In the long period of the Romans, from 753 B.C. to A.D. 476, Italy became the richest and most powerful nation in the ancient world, ruling a vast empire. But when the northern barbarian invaders overran Europe in the fifth century A.D., Italy changed like the rest of Europe into warring feudal principalities, some no bigger than many American villages. There was no longer any central government in Italy; instead, chaos and ignorance reigned. For centuries she was cut off from discovery, trade, and learning. The statues and stadiums of ancient Rome fell into disrepair. Old manuscripts full of the vast knowledge of the ancient world lay buried and forgotten.

Then, first of all the countries in Europe, Italy began to shake off the dust of the Middle Ages and to feel the call of a new way of life. The crusades, starting at the end of the eleventh century, opened up trade routes in the Mediterranean. Italian merchants rapidly developed a prosperous trade between East and West.

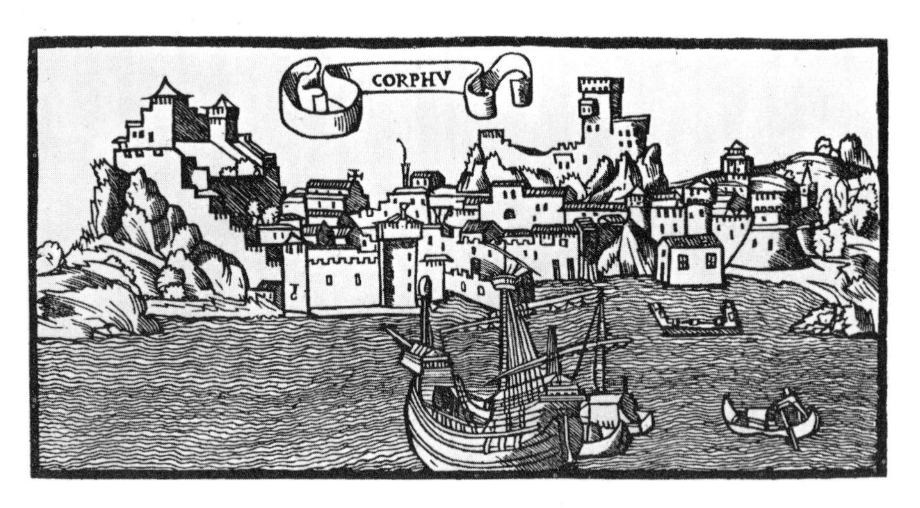

Venetian galley at Corfu, one of her island possessions in the Mediterranean.

The ruins of the great Roman amphitheater, the Colosseum.

Silks and spices from the East were loaded on Italian ships and unloaded at Italian ports. As wealth began to pour into Italy, so did the realization that life could be gayer, freer, and more beautiful. While the barons of northern Europe were fighting and quarreling among themselves in a most feudal way, Italy outgrew feudalism. Her merchants became powerful and controlled the towns, which in turn grew so large that they expanded into city-states, owning neighboring lands and even colonies as far away as the Black Sea.

Italy had another advantage besides her location on wealthy sea routes. Because she had once been the Roman center of the world, the remains of those great days were still about, though neglected. Ruins of theaters, aqueducts, roads, lovely statues and columns and marble ornaments were constant reminders of past glories. People began to look with new eyes at the sunken foundations of Roman buildings, now used as cow pastures and quarries. With feverish excitement they began to dig under the rubble and dust for ancient works of art and to hunt for ancient manuscripts, as if to say, "Wake up and see the glories of our past!" This was the very beginning of what we call the Italian Renaissance.

Italy had still another connection with the past which gave her a claim to importance. Throughout the centuries following the fall of the Roman Empire, the city of Rome nevertheless remained the religious center of the Christian world. The Popes were the spiritual leaders of Europe. As the Renaissance developed, they too became interested in the revival of learning and were great patrons of the new literature and art. Nicholas V, who ruled in the middle of the fifteenth century, was the first Renaissance Pope. He spent most of his money on books and manuscripts; he was enraptured with the newly rediscovered classics. But besides making Rome into a center of beauty and culture, he also expanded it into a grand and powerful city-state.

At the same time, four other Italian states were growing particularly strong and ambitious: Venice, Milan, Naples, and Florence. These states were rivals for power and prestige. Each one wanted to have the finest university, the most elaborate buildings, the most famous painters and sculptors and poets.

Venice, in the north, developed into a seafaring empire that stretched across the Adriatic Sea and into Greece and the Greek islands. Its city of many islands and canals and hundreds of bridges and colorful marble palaces stunned all visitors with its splendor. Its festivals were renowned throughout Europe.

Milan, in the fertile valley of the Po River, was a worthy competitor. Continually at war with Venice and combinations of other Italian states, it too in the fifteenth century rose to great wealth and strength. The tyrants who ruled Milan collected works of art as well as the heads of their opponents.

Naples had the largest territory of all the states on the Italian Peninsula. It was not as rich as the other great states, for its peasants had a hard time raising crops and animals on its harsh soil. But because of its size and its alliances with foreign nations it was a continual threat to other Italian lands.

The fifth of these big states, Florence, was in the center of Italy. Of all the Italian city-states, Florence was the first to feel the awakening of the Renaissance. Its citizens, eager for learning and beauty of all sorts, built a magical city, matchless even today in the splendor of its achievement. All of Italy, and later all of Europe—and even later the New World across the Atlantic—inherited much of its culture from Florence, the greatest of Renaissance cities.

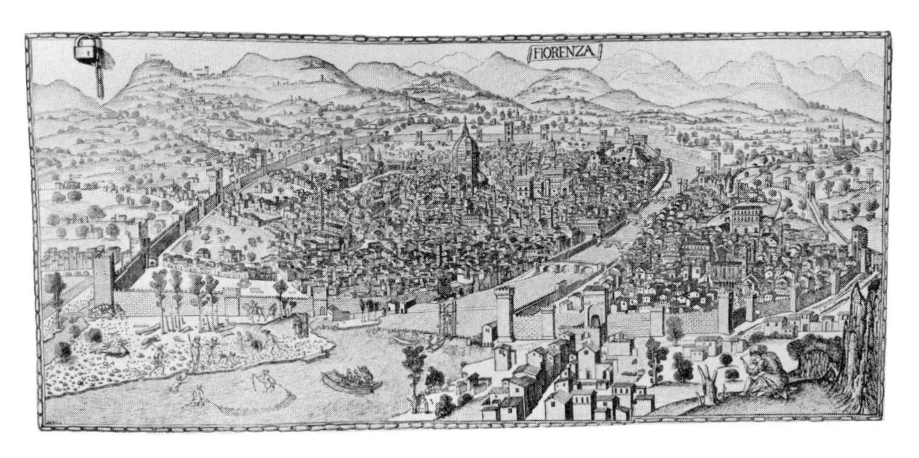

The walled city of Florence in Lorenzo's time.

BETTMAN ARCHIVES

LORENZO DE MEDICI

Lorenzo de' Medici. Terra-cotta head by Verrocchio.

NATIONAL GALLERY OF ART, WASHINGTON

LORENZO DE' MEDICI was born in the beautiful Italian city-state of Florence in the middle of the fifteenth century. His contemporaries called him Lorenzo il Magnifico (Lorenzo the Magnificent) because he was so many things—ruler, scholar, millionaire, athlete, musician, poet, diplomat, and patron of such extraordinary artists as Michelangelo, Botticelli, and Leonardo da Vinci. He was to the people of his day and to us today the perfect example of the

Renaissance man: the man who wanted to do all things and to know all things. "Men can do all things if they will," said a citizen of Florence who lived in those exciting times. This was a new and inspiring concept which encouraged men like Lorenzo to attempt things that would have been thought impossible in the Middle Ages.

In Italy at the time of Lorenzo's birth there were many other rulers who had great gifts and varied interests—from wise and scholarly Pope Nicholas V, who made Rome a center of culture once more, to the athletic tyrant Francesco Sforza of Milan, who rebuilt his city and encouraged education. Even the smallest walled principality in Renaissance Italy was likely to be ruled by a man who, though he might be plotting a political murder, collected rare manuscripts at the same time.

All the towns and territories in Italy benefited from the enthusiasm of their educated rulers, who used their wealth to endow artists and scholars and to build libraries and universities. Nowhere was this truer than in Lorenzo's Florence. Under his inspired guidance the city-state was to rise to its greatest glory and become an example to all Europe.

When Lorenzo was born, the city-state of Florence was already big and rich. It controlled the seaport of Pisa and many other towns. Forests and castles and villas on outlying hills were part of its domain. Its trade was widespread, its banking and industry famous. Its central city showed the influence of the great architects and artists who were lured by the fame and the pay that its citizens so gladly gave. The huge red octagonal dome of the Cathedral, a marvelous architectural novelty of the Renaissance, dominated the city. The Baptistery, the building where children were baptized, had eight high bronze doors, so beautifully ornamented with favorite biblical scenes and characters that they were called the "gates of Paradise." The great square was full of statues and surrounded by buildings on whose walls brilliant pictures were painted, each building more spectacular than the next. Some were ten stories high and the tips of their towers could be seen for many miles across the nearby hills and plains. And on many buildings fluttered the flag of Lorenzo's grandfather, Cosimo de' Medici, a wealthy banker and the ruler of Florence.

Lorenzo in his youth, accompanied by other rich boys in elegant clothes, loved to run and dodge through the colorful crowds that thronged the busy streets—soldiers with pike and clumsy arquebus; cardinals of the Church in scarlet robes; bejeweled ladies with dyed yellow hair. Strong turbaned slaves from oriental lands carried heavy baskets of pungent spices to the markets of the city. Laborers wheeled newly excavated statues on barrows through the streets to some wealthy merchant's garden. Scholars in long robes hurried to the Academy with the latest classical translations under their arms. The sounds of the goldsmith's hammer, the architect yelling at the stonecutters, the banging of the looms making the city's famous woolen cloth—these were daily music to young Lorenzo's ears.

The citizens of the city-state affectionately watched Lorenzo grow up. They knew that he would soon be their ruler, for his grandfather was an old man and his father a semi-invalid. From the first, Lorenzo won all hearts by his friendly, open disposition. People from every walk of life were drawn to him and his gay, handsome younger brother Giuliano. Lorenzo, with his turned-up, twisted nose, was rather ugly, but this did not matter, for he had great charm. Both brothers were fine athletes and expert riders. The townspeople cheered them as they joined street football games or wild-animal hunts staged in the public square, or tournaments with lance and sword. At all these sports they excelled. In one tournament Lorenzo, mounted on a magnificent horse, wore a helmet of silver and carried a shield with a great diamond in it. He was declared the winner, "not by favor, but by his own valor." Both boys loved laughter and songs and the parades and carnivals for which the Medici family commissioned the greatest artists and sculptors of the day to design elaborate costumes and floats.

Like all children of good Renaissance families, Lorenzo and his brother had to have a complete education. This was typical of the new times. No more could boys be brought up like young knights of the Middle Ages, who studied little and read less. Now that the

Young Lorenzo in a procession. From a fresco in the Medici Palace

ALINARI PHOTO

revival of learning was sweeping Italy and the great works of the ancients were being rediscovered, there were exciting things to read on every subject from astronomy to poetry. Lorenzo and Giuliano learned Greek and Latin in order to read these works. They discussed philosophy and wrote poetry—Lorenzo even became one of the best poets of the age. They learned to write music, play the lute, and sing their own songs. Their religious education was strict, too, for in those days every Christian had a thorough Roman Catholic upbringing. They were also taught how to dance gracefully. They learned swordsmanship and the arts of war.

The boys were brought up in their grandfather's palace, the latest, newest house that the Renaissance architects could possibly design. It was far more modern than the other palaces of Europe. Other nations were still building the thick, towered, almost windowless castles of the Middle Ages; but times were changing, and the old castles were soon to be considered out of date. The Medici palace stood in the middle of the city, but instead of having a moat around it and a drawbridge, it had a stone bench for the townspeople to sit on, and an open courtyard where outsiders could walk in and mingle with Lorenzo's family. On its roof there were no warlike battlements, but an elegant wide cornice of elaborate stone. The windows were large and the rooms were light and gay, filled with art treasures. Lorenzo could wander from room to room, looking at exquisite paintings, furniture carved and inlaid with precious woods, dishes and goblets of gold and crystal.

Banquet and gay company in 15th Century Florence.

THE METROPOLITAN MUSEUM OF ART, NEW YORK

Everywhere the Medici palace was known as the "Hotel of Princes and All the World." It was jammed with people. The large Medici family of three generations was a mere fraction of the crowd the palace housed. Painters, sculptors, and scholars were always being invited to live with the family. Visiting princes or ambassadors or cardinals—with their huge retinues—would naturally stay there. All these people had to be fed and waited upon by many servants. Yet Lorenzo often helped at the great tables, for his grandfather believed that in spite of all his wealth his grandson should be brought up to serve others.

The Medici family also owned villas in the lovely countryside to which they often retired from the bustle of the town. Placed among gentle hills surrounded by farms and woods and streams, with gardens and orchards nearby, these villas too were lavishly decorated by popular artists. Lorenzo and Giuliano spent many months of their boyhood at these villas, hunting and hawking, watching their mother direct the making of cheeses and olive oil and the weaving of linen sheets.

When Lorenzo was only fifteen his grandfather died, and a few years later his ailing father died too.

Now Lorenzo found himself the richest and most powerful man in Florence. He had to manage the complex, enormous family business. In addition, he had to run the government of the state.

This was a difficult and dangerous job. The big city-state had strong competitors among the other thriving states of the Italian Peninsula—particularly Milan, Venice, Rome, and Naples—any of which might combine and attack him at any time. Each one wanted more territory and power and would quickly attack a weak neighbor. It was Lorenzo's first care to see that Florence should not be swallowed up by these other states. He had an additional worry: countries outside of Italy, like Spain or France, were becoming big nations instead of weak combinations of quarreling little states. Their armies were growing and so were their imperialistic ambitions. Another terrible threat was the Turks, now gobbling up Christian territories to the west of Constantinople, which they had captured soon after Lorenzo's birth. Every year the Turks were getting nearer to the Italian shores. Lorenzo knew that only a peaceful, united Italy could resist these powerful invaders. Peace among the selfish, turbulent Italian states was the dream of his life.

A famous Florentine sculptor, Verrocchio, made a terra-cotta head of Lorenzo which gives us a good idea of how he looked at this time. His hair is thick, his forehead wide and intelligent, his jaw strong. The end of his thin long nose is twisted to one side. His mouth is half smiling, half severe. The whole impression is one of both power and benevolence, for, like all Renaissance rulers, he could change quickly from a generous and charming friend into a stern ruler, merciless to his enemies.

And enemies he had, in spite of his careful rule and noble ideals. Jealous merchants within Florence envied his wealth and political power. Neighboring tyrants wanted to be free of Florence's control and would stop at no bloody deed to achieve this end. In those days cruelty went hand in hand with beauty. One Renaissance duke trained dogs to eat the flesh of his political prisoners. Another was stabbed in his bedroom by assassins hired by his wife. Rivals were thrown out of high windows to the pavements below. No one even lifted an eyebrow at the legal punishments of the day—blinding or branding or strangling or burning at the stake. It was inevitable in such an age that someone would think it advantageous to murder Lorenzo. The threat of assassination by some dissatisfied or ambitious person always haunted him.

Even the new Pope, Sixtus IV, who perhaps should have had his mind on holier subjects, was an enemy of Lorenzo and wanted him removed. Popes in those days were often more politicians than churchmen. Their courts were as elaborate as any in the land, and they too were great patrons of artists and scholars. Riches poured into Rome from the Catholic countries of Europe. Popes had troops and made military alliances with both Italian city-states and foreign countries. There were six different Popes within Lorenzo's lifetime, but only Sixtus was his enemy.

Pope Sixtus was a warrior, a scholar, and a politician. He loved power and wanted to expand the papal territories. He gave lands and money to his relatives, who spent the money wildly and ruled the lands foolishly. When he bought a city near the southern border of Florence and handed it over to a favorite nephew, he ran head-on into Lorenzo, who wanted the same city as a buffer between himself and the Pope's designs. A conflict was bound to

A favorite country villa of the Medici family.

BETTMAN ARCHIVES

come. Then the Pope insultingly sent another particularly hateful young nephew as archbishop within Lorenzo's own territory. Lorenzo was enraged. He tried by every means to make trouble for the Pope's nephews, even using troops to prevent the new archbishop from getting near his new district.

Now it was a contest of wills. The Pope removed his bulging money sacks from the Medici bank and gave them to a rival Florentine bank run by the jealous, conniving Pazzi family. Lorenzo in revenge tried to ruin the Pazzi banking business.

Pope Sixtus IV and his nephews.

BETTMANN ARCHIVES

Soon the Pazzi family and the Pope's nephews combined in common hatred of Lorenzo and plotted to get rid of him. They told the Pope of their intention. As a churchman, he professed horror at murder, but as a politician, he urged them to remove Lorenzo from his path. Assassination was so common in Renaissance days that Sixtus knew very well the conspirators would not get rid of Lorenzo by any other method. At the end of their interview with Pope Sixtus, the conspirators promised that he would soon be in control of Florence and half of Italy.

Then they quickly planned the murderous details. Both Lorenzo and Giuliano would have to be disposed of, for the assassins realized that unless both were killed the survivor would wreak dreadful revenge for the death of his beloved brother. They worked out a most unholy plot—on a holy day in a holy place.

Easter Day arrived—sunny and pleasant, but soon to be cloudy and bloody. The high bells of Florence rang and the doors of the city houses opened. People in their fanciest clothes thronged to the Cathedral. The sun shone gaily on its big dome and streamed through its high windows, shining on the heads of the worshipers, priests, and choir. Arriving early, the murderers saw that Lorenzo was in his usual place up front, near the choir—but his brother Giuliano had not arrived, and they dared not go ahead with their plan unless he appeared. Quickly two assassins, the young Pazzi son and a friend, went to look for him. When they caught up with him, a thought occurred to them: what if Giuliano were wearing chain mail beneath his elegant silks? So young Francesco Pazzi gave him a friendly slap on the back, felt to his relief only muscles instead of mail, and urged him to hurry. Laughing and joking, the three entered the Cathedral.

Giuliano took his customary place in the forefront of the crowd and the assassins stood next to him. Lorenzo was standing some distance away.

At a most solemn moment in the ceremony, while the colorful company was hushed beneath the majestic dome, the murderers fell upon their victims. The young and handsome Giuliano was struck savagely, again and again. Though the first blow nearly killed him, he was stabbed eighteen more times. The murderer Francesco Pazzi slashed at him so furiously that he cut his own leg badly and could barely make his getaway.

Meanwhile two priests attacked Lorenzo, but they were not as accomplished murderers as the two civilians, and gave him merely a glancing blow on the shoulder. Lorenzo quickly realized what was happening. He wrapped his heavy cloak around his arm as a shield, pulled out his sword, and vaulted lightly over the choir rail. His brother's murderers pursued him, knowing they could not afford to let him escape. But a friend of Lorenzo's, a famous poet, immediately clanged the heavy sacristy doors behind him and saved his life. Another friend sucked the dagger wound in his shoulder in case the weapon had been poisoned. Under their protection Lorenzo moved swiftly through the streets to the Medici palace. Giuliano's bleeding body was soon carried there too. The city, rocked by horror and confusion, was in an uproar—but rallied solidly behind Lorenzo instead of revolting against the Medici "tyrant" as the hopeful conspirators had planned.

When the plotting archbishop, the Pope's nephew, tried to take over the government, he found a strong chain stretched across the wide stairway of the government building, while its great bell clanged frantically to summon the loyal people. As he pulled futilely at the chain, an enraged mob caught him and hanged him in all his ornate vestments from the high windows. Francesco Pazzi, writhing from the leg wound that he had made with his own wild jabbing, met the same fate. Some followers of the archbishop were tossed out of the windows into the courtyard. Others were hanged from the same windows. A craze for vengeance seized the city until almost everyone connected with the crime paid for it with his life. In all, some eighty persons were killed by mob violence.

The head of the Pazzi family, an old man, tried to escape to the countryside, but peasants loyal to the Medici would not be bribed to hide him. As was the custom, he was tortured before he was executed. Then, in each of the four corners of the city, his old body was hung from a tree and whipped, until finally an unrecognizable lump of flesh was thrown into the city's swift, flooding river. People watched silently from every bridge as the last victim of the unsuccessful conspiracy was swept beneath them toward the sea.

This savagery and brutality were characteristic of Renaissance days. But just as characteristic was the artistic commemoration of the event. A young Florentine painter, Botticelli, was immediately commissioned to paint in fresco on the prison walls a picture of all the principal conspirators hanging by their necks

A burning in the great Square of Florence, fifteenth century.

BETTMANN ARCHIVES

from the windows. Lorenzo himself wrote the verses beneath each ghastly portrait. Passers-by were reminded many times of that terrible day.

Giuliano was given a lavish funeral, and huge crowds mourned this man who had contributed so much to the gaiety of the city. Lorenzo's hold on the city increased and his popularity was never greater.

When Pope Sixtus heard that his archbishop had been hanged and that Lorenzo was still alive, he excommunicated Lorenzo, calling him a son of iniquity and a child of perdition. Then the martial Pope declared war.

As usual, this involved other Italian states, for the Pope did not have a big enough army of his own. His most powerful ally was the fierce and opportunistic King of Naples, to the south. Both men hired the best mercenary troops they could find and ordered them to march northward through the mountainous land to Florence. They laid waste to Lorenzo's fertile countryside and brought famine and disease. In a year they stood within eight miles of the city's walls.

The situation was desperate for Lorenzo and for his city. His people had been taxed severely to pay for defense and soon the money to pay the army would run out. Some way must be found to conclude a peace with honor.

Lorenzo now did a heroic thing. He went secretly, alone and unarmed, by boat to the court of his enemy, the King of Naples. This king had just murdered another diplomatic visitor. Whether he would murder Lorenzo or not remained to be seen. But Lorenzo was willing to risk everything for his little country. The Florentines did not know of his mission until he had left, for Lorenzo knew that they would not let him go on such a hazardous undertaking. He sent them a letter just after he had set out, which they received with tears and consternation:

"Perhaps God wills that this war, which began in the blood of my brother and myself, should be ended by my means. My desire is that by my life or my death I may contribute to the well-being of our city. Should I be successful I shall rejoice in having won peace for my country . . . should I fail, I shall know that my misfortunes were necessary for our city's good."

King Ferrante of Naples, impressed by Lorenzo's appearance and his courage, listened to his arguments for peace. Lorenzo pointed out that a strong Pope in possession of the riches and lands of Florence would be a dangerous neighbor to the king. He then mentioned a worse threat—the Turks. Now, in 1480, these fierce Moslems had reached the Adriatic Sea and were advancing dangerously near the Italian coast. If the Italian states were fighting each other, said Lorenzo, they might fall easy prey to the Turkish foe.

For three months Lorenzo was a well-treated prisoner at the court of the King of Naples. His countrymen at home were frantic, wondering if he would return alive. But Lorenzo's good manners, charm, and cleverness had their usual effect. To the chagrin of the Pope, King Ferrante signed a peace treaty and sent Lorenzo home on a fine horse with the treaty in his hand.

That year the Turks actually set foot on Italian soil. The Pope had to forgive Lorenzo in order to have his support against the Mohammedans. Along with his forgiveness came the request for fifteen Florentine galleys—slim fighting ships with slaves at their rows of oars—for use against the Turks. Soon the Turks were forced to retreat.

Thus the peace that Lorenzo wanted came to Italy. In the twelve years which were left to him he became a mediator again and again among the conflicting Italian states, for other rulers trusted his motives and respected his judgment. His dream of a strong Italy, no longer fighting within itself, seemed possible at last. He befriended the new Pope, Innocent VIII, for this time he wanted to be sure to be on good terms with powerful Rome. He often sent the Pope special red wine, the finest damask cloth, and little birds for his dinner. He made alliances with the new King of France and with King Ferdinand and Queen Isabella of Spain, for his spies told him that both these increasingly powerful nations had their eyes on rich Italy. Lorenzo realized that it was no longer enough to be a good Florentine, but that one had also to be a good Italian in order to defend Italy's marvelous heritage.

The last twelve years of his rule were happy and prosperous for Italy. The merchants became wealthier, and the people, now briefly at peace, had jobs and food.

Now Lorenzo could turn to the things he loved best. Artists and writers, poets and scholars flocked to his court, knowing that he would give them friendship, encouragement, and money. Florence became the cultural center of the Western world. So frequently was classical Greek heard in the streets that Florence was compared to ancient Athens. The best thinkers came to its academies, the best musicians to its choirs. Other rich Florentine families besides the Medici built palaces and villas, luring artists to paint frescoes on the walls and to carve statues for their gardens. Churches and civic buildings became as elegant and beautiful as private palaces. The people of Florence were proud of their artists and philosophers, and eager to hire and reward them.

The Medici palace was like a museum, bursting with Lorenzo's collections of the latest paintings, bronzes, porcelains, coins, and gems. Its library swelled into one of the finest of the day, for Lorenzo sent scouts to buy ancient manuscripts whenever he

Michelangelo's David.

ALINARI PHOTO

heard of a newly discovered one. He hired translators to work on these manuscripts, turning Greek into Latin or Italian. That revolutionary Renaissance invention, the printing press, came to Florence in 1471, and Lorenzo's library grew more speedily than in the days of copying by hand.

Lorenzo had a special garden for sculpture, particularly for the Greek and Roman statues dug up from long-buried courtyards or discovered in deserted ruins. He invited young sculptors to study them. These students were excited and inspired by the beauty of the statues, and relieved that they no longer had to use as models the rather stiff, wooden-looking religious figures of the Middle Ages. The lifelike, graceful sculpture of an even earlier age seemed fresh and wonderful as they studied them in Lorenzo's garden.

One day, while strolling through this garden, Lorenzo found a boy with a chisel, copying the head of a faun. He was struck with the boy's ability, and perhaps guessing that he might one day become a great sculptor, invited him to live at the Medici palace. The boy's name was Michelangelo. He dined every midday at the long Medici table where Lorenzo always sat with his children and guests, allowing anyone who got there first to sit next to him, no matter how young or unimportant. Every day Michelangelo showed his work to Lorenzo, who by his encouragement started him on his road to success.

Another young artist under Lorenzo's patronage for a while was Leonardo da Vinci, eventually to flower into the most amazing genius of the Renaissance. Botticelli, a brilliant painter who did many works for Lorenzo and the Medici circle, was another.

Scholars, philosophers, and poets were Lorenzo's great friends. He spent long hours with them. When the cares of government were too heavy, he would find relaxation in writing poetry of all kinds—from carnival songs to serious sonnets, as fine as any poet's of the day. One of his favorite subjects was the Italian countryside, which he described in the lovely soft Italian tongue:

> Un verde praticel pien di bei fiori,
> Un rivolo che l'erba intorno bagni . . .
>
> L'ombre selve, i sassi e gli alti monti
> Gli antri oscuri, e le fere fuggitive. . . .
>
> A green meadow full of lovely flowers,
> A stream which washes the grass on its banks . . .
>
> The leafy woods, the rocks, the high hills,
> The dark caves, the wild animals in flight. . . .

Lorenzo retired more and more to his favorite country villas. Here he added to his hobbies, as if he did not have enough already, and became fascinated with agricultural experiments. He also used one villa as a small zoo, for the Sultan of Babylon had sent him apes and parrots and a giraffe "so gentle that it would take an apple from the hand of a child."

Lorenzo's seven children grew up in the midst of splendor and variety. He arranged their future with care and strengthened the family fortunes by making important marriages for them. He trained his first son in the complicated role of ruling Florence. Having been almost ruined by a Pope in his own youth, he wanted to be sure to have a Medici of the next generation in the inner circles of Rome, and so managed with money and diplomacy to have his second son made a cardinal of the Church—at age thirteen! This boy was later to become a Pope, Leo X.

As Lorenzo grew older he suffered from gout and arthritis. His health began to decline. One day in his country villa pains seized him. So primitive was medicine in those days, when so much else was advancing, that the best cure the doctors could prescribe was a mixture of jewels ground to powder. Somehow this failed to work. His friends and family surrounded him and he made his last farewells, dying with a silver crucifix pressed to his lips. He was only forty-three.

There was mourning for him throughout the civilized world, for people of all lands and ranks had held him in affection and esteem. The King of Naples, his old enemy, said that Lorenzo had lived long enough for his glory, but too short a time for Italy.

In the fall of the year that Lorenzo died, Columbus discovered America for Spain. The fortunes of the world soon turned from the Mediterranean to the countries that faced the Atlantic. Spain and France and England became powerful nations. Italy started internal fighting once more. Its riches declined and foreign armies occupied its soil.

Yet these foreign conquerors learned a great deal from Italy. They were amazed at the treasures of the civilization of the great Italian rulers, Popes, and patrons. They copied not only Italian dress and manners, but its houses and palaces, for theirs suddenly seemed crude in contrast. Italian paintings and statues, architecture and furniture became the rage of Europe. Italian translations of ancient Greek and Roman stories and plays were eagerly read and copied by writers of other nations. Italian tutors came to foreign courts to teach the new way of life; Italian artists lived and painted at foreign courts. Each European city tried to be a second Florence, and each ruler a second Lorenzo de' Medici. Thus the learning of the Italians spread, and gradually all of Europe felt the influence of the Italian Renaissance.

Botticelli's Venus.

ALINARI PHOTO

LEONARDO DA VINCI

Self-portrait of Leonardo da Vinci as an old man.

ALINARI PHOTO

"OCCASIONALLY Heaven sends someone who is not only human but divine so that through his mind and the excellence of his intellect we may reach out to Heaven." So wrote the Italian historian, Vasari, about Leonardo da Vinci, who lived at the peak of the Renaissance in Lorenzo's Golden Age. Leonardo da Vinci was a man of so many talents and interests that it is hard to know whether to call him artist, sculptor, scientist, engineer, or philosopher. Actually he was all these rolled into one extraordinary person, a genius and a man ahead of his time. The comments of his contemporaries testify to the fame he had in his lifetime. He still holds a fascination for modern man.

What proof have we that this man who lived five hundred years ago was so extraordinary? He completed only a few paintings, but at least two of them—the *Mona Lisa* and *The Last Supper*—are world-famous. He left many wonderful drawings and sketches, some in preparation for these paintings, others to record the multitude of things in which he was interested, from the anatomy of man to the swirling waters of a flood. Finally there are Leonardo's notebooks in which he recorded his theory of painting and many of his discoveries and inventions.

His notebooks deal with almost any subject you can think of: observations on nature, the flight of birds, water, air, art and perspective, war machines and guns. They describe intricate waterways, canals, and tunnels, submarines and diving suits; they even deal with anatomy, astronomy, and the soul of man. All these ideas, with explanations, are written in mirror writing, written with his left hand from right to left, as though he did not wish the world to read them. Was this because he did not feel they were ready for the world to see or because he did not think the world was ready for them? We do not know, though we do know that he hoped to put them in order, in book form, but never found the time.

Leonardo was a perfectionist, always striving to do better and never satisfied with his own work. At the end of his life he said bitterly, "I have never completed a single work." It is true that Leonardo left many things unfinished, a new interest compelling him to go on to something else he considered more important. He annoyed his patrons by his slowness and by working on several projects at one time. But many of his works of art which did not satisfy him are to us, and were to his admirers then, perfection itself.

Leonardo was born in 1452 in the small town of Vinci, outside of Florence. The lovely, olive-colored Tuscan hills, rocky cliffs, and clear streams in wide valleys are nearly the same today as they were in Leonardo's youth. He spent much of his early boyhood climbing these hills, exploring caves and observing nature. As a boy Leonardo showed an insatiable curiosity about everything. He learned far more from his own observations of nature and his own experiences than he ever did at school.

He wanted to find out things for himself, how and why things worked the way they did. In one of his wanderings among the hills near Vinci he found sea shells and fishbones embedded in a rocky cave. How did these creatures from the sea ever get into a cave high up in the Tuscan hills? This kind of question interested Leonardo more than learning to write or add numbers.

Leonardo collected animals, insects, lizards, and snakes and kept them in his room to observe their habits. Once when asked by his father to decorate an old wooden shield, he used these creatures as models. Shutting himself up in his room, he set to work enthusiastically. His imagination conceived a sort of dragon as decoration for the shield. It had the head of one animal, the body of another, and the eyes and tail of a third. This horrible monster was breathing fire and smoke. Leonardo placed the finished shield in a corner of his darkened room. As his father opened the door, the light fell upon the lifelike dragon and his father drew back in terror.

In 1469, when Leonardo was about seventeen, his family moved to Florence and apprenticed him to a master artist, Andrea del Verrocchio, the most esteemed master of arts in the city.

Verrocchio's studio was a typical Renaissance workshop and Verrocchio was a typical Renaissance artist: craftsman, sculptor, painter, and goldsmith. Verrocchio's pupils lived with him and worked in his studio, learning all sorts of crafts, of which painting was one. An artist was not specialized then as he is now and was expected to learn not only to paint and sculpture, but also to cast metals and set precious jewels in gold. He had to make his own paints by extracting pigments from plants or minerals and grinding them into powders. Leonardo with his insatiable curiosity soon learned how to do all these things.

But it was Leonardo's talented drawings which first impressed his master. Leonardo seemed to grasp the theory of perspective, a new idea at the time, exceedingly well. In the Middle Ages painting had been flat and unreal, objects near and far being of equal size. Medieval artists did not know how to draw things so that some appeared to be near and others far away. Mathematics and geometry were needed to understand the laws of perspective. Leonardo, now seeing a need for mathematics, plunged into Verrocchio's geometry books with such enthusiasm and asked such searching questions that he astounded his master.

The apprentices at Verrocchio's studio were also experimenting with a new kind of paint. The pigments were mixed with oil and used on canvas or wood panels. In the Middle Ages painters had painted in tempera—colors mixed with egg yolk. Tempera gave clear, bright colors but dried fast and was not easy to handle. A northern artist, Jan Van Eyck, discovered that oil could be used instead of egg yolk. Oil did not harm the bright colors and oil paint went on wood or canvas more easily and smoothly. Also it dried slowly and allowed an artist plenty of time to think as he painted.

There is a story that while at Verrocchio's studio Leonardo was asked to add an angel to a painting on which his master was working. The angel proved to be the best part of the picture. Verrocchio was so amazed that his young pupil could excel him, the old master, that he decided never to paint another picture. Today this painting, *The Baptism of Christ,* with Leonardo's lovely angel, hangs in the Uffizi Gallery in Florence.

Leonardo astounded not only his master but other artists of the day. He also charmed people by his courteous ways and good looks. He had golden flowing hair, penetrating blue eyes, and a fine build. Though his hands looked delicate, they were strong enough to bend an iron horseshoe. He usually wore a short rose-colored tunic. He was always neat and well groomed, and dressed in simple elegance, not in lavish splendor. He had a lovely musical voice and could play the lute with great skill.

As this boy grew to manhood his interests and curiosity deepened. A perfectionist, he wanted every detail of his paintings to be

Baptism of Christ. The angel at left is by Leonardo.

ALINARI PHOTO

true to life. He would study how the wind blows wheat in a field or just what muscles of the face contract or expand to cause a smile or a frown. He studied the effects of light and shade to make his work more real.

His interest in mathematics led him on to physics and the laws of nature: how fish swim; how birds fly; how sound spreads; what causes waves; what is motion. He remembered the fish fossils in the mountain cave and he wondered if it were possible that what were now mountains were once at the bottom of the sea. Had streams and rivers, carrying soil and rocks to the sea, finally built up land so that sea became land and land became sea? He discussed these ideas with the aged astronomer and map maker, Toscanelli. He asked questions about clouds and winds and the age of the earth, questions which had not been asked before.

All these questions and ideas he jotted down in his strange, backward writing. Like a modern scientist, Leonardo believed in experimenting; one must try things out and experience them before arriving at a conclusion. He made designs for a telescope which he never perfected but he observed the stars, the planets and moon with considerable accuracy. He came to the then startling conclusion that the sun does not move and that the earth is not the center of the universe. A hundred years later Galileo, an Italian scientist, would prove this to the world.

Some of Leonardo's experiments resulted in everyday, practical inventions such as scissors which would open and shut with one movement of the hand, a machine for sharpening needles, a machine for cutting threads on a screw and even, though perhaps not so practical, inflated skis for walking on water.

Leonardo was not above making toys and gadgets for practical jokes. There is a tale of how he stupefied his friends by taking the entrails of a sheep and blowing air into them until they reached such a size that the whole room was filled by this strange "balloon." His terrified friends were flattened against the wall.

Years later, to amuse the fat, joke-loving Pope Leo X, Leonardo devised many odd toys. Upon finding an unusual lizard, he attached scaly wings, horns, and a beard. With quicksilver he made its wings flutter. The Pope was delighted to see this strange lizard pop out of a box and terrify his guests.

Florentine artists were noted for their practical jokes. When Leonardo dined with his sculptor friend, Rustici, a tree suddenly rose up through the floor. Its branches, laden with food and dishes, swung over the table, handing each guest his food!

After seven years' apprenticeship with Verrocchio, Leonardo was invited to join the famous Medici group of artists. But for some reason Italy's greatest Renaissance art patron, Lorenzo, did not give him many assignments. It is true that Leonardo was not easy to do business with, for he often failed to complete his work on time. Whatever the reason, Leonardo did not have many commissions in Florence and when he had an opportunity to seek his fortune in the rich city-state of Milan he seized it. He had heard that Milan's ruler, Lodovico Sforza, wanted an engineer, an architect, and a painter. And so Leonardo wrote to Lodovico, telling of his many accomplishments: of his inventions of war machines, armored cars or tanks, new kinds of movable cannon and bridges, all kinds of engines for attack and defense. He added that he had plans for intricate waterways and canals and new designs for buildings, and at the end he said, "I can execute sculpture in marble, bronze or clay and also painting in which my work will stand comparison with that of anyone whosoever he be."

Lorenzo de' Medici was glad to give Leonardo a letter of introduction to the Duke of Milan and, as was the custom, he sent along a gift. The gift, an unusual creation by Leonardo himself, was a silver lute fashioned in the shape of a horse's skull, with the teeth used for pegs to tune the strings. Its odd shape gave it a louder and more sonorous tone than that of an ordinary lute.

Leonardo also took with him a more precious work of art, his lovely *Virgin of the Rocks,* which now hangs in the Louvre in Paris. The beautiful forms of the Madonna, the Christ child and angel are set against one of Leonardo's typical backgrounds with strange rock formations, waterfalls, and mists. His clever use of light and shadow, which softened features and made the whole picture flow together, set his art apart from that of other painters of the time.

In 1482, Leonardo arrived in Milan and was warmly welcomed by Lodovico. He charmed the great court by his exquisite voice and his skill on the lute. Lodovico, called Il Moro (the Moor) because of his dark complexion, had usurped the power and been made Duke of Milan. Full of the new learning and interest in ancient classics, he, like Lorenzo, surrounded himself with famous scholars, poets, and artists. He was ambitious to make Milan the richest, most powerful, and most learned center of all Italy. The city itself had grown in wealth, through its wonderful silk and cloth industries, to equal Florence. The armorers' guilds were the most famous in Europe, producing beautiful and highly decorated armor. The duke's palace, the great castello, was the largest and grandest in Italy, but its heavy fortifications deprived it of the beauty and simplicity of the Medici palace in Florence. The Cathe-

The Virgin of the Rocks by Leonardo.

ALINARI PHOTO

dral, of pure white marble, massive and ornate, was nearing completion.

When Leonardo came to Milan the city was at its peak of wealth and power. The Renaissance was bursting forth in this northern Italian city with a lavishness and splendor hitherto unknown. For a brief decade the glory of the Renaissance passed from Florence to Milan. Its court was becoming the most dazzling not only of Italy but of all Europe. Duke Lodovico, though not as literary or as discriminating as Lorenzo de' Medici, was a most generous patron of art. He loved music and his court was filled with musicians as well as poets. Dancing and masked balls were frequent. All forms of art filled his castello: rich carpets from the East, Greek and Roman statues, and paintings by artists of the day.

The duke was quick to recognize Leonardo's many talents, though at first he hired him more as a mechanic and scenery designer than as a true artist. For a famous ball the duke commissioned Leonardo to design the scenery and costumes. This was not unusual at the time. Artists were just as often hired to design scenery, jewelry, and costumes as to paint Madonnas and saints. This was certainly not new to Leonardo, who had had a hand in decorations and costumes for the colorful tournaments staged by Lorenzo and other wealthy citizens of Florence.

There had been months of preparation for this ball, the Paradise Festival as it was later to be known. The city buzzed with excitement and anticipation. What costumes would there be, what strange and wonderful inventions would that man from Florence, Leonardo da Vinci, turn out for the guests to wonder at?

The huge ducal palace was gaily lighted when the guests from far and near began to arrive. Many came in heavy gilded wagons drawn by brightly caparisoned horses. As the guests—ladies in brocaded and bejeweled gowns, men in brightly colored satins and velvets—alighted, they made their way through a long passage lined with armed guards. These soldiers, Turkish, Swiss, and German, glittered in their shining armor. Handsome young pages in particolored liveries, one leg pink and one leg blue, held aloft huge candelabra to light the guests' way into the palace. As each guest entered the hall, a herald attended by two trumpeters proclaimed his title and his rank.

The duke, in brocaded mantle trimmed with ermine and sparkling jewels, felt proud. He was now the wealthiest ruler in all Italy and had the most sumptuous court. By his side stood the court poet, Bellincioni, who was ready with rhymed verses of praise for the great duke.

At midnight the curtains were drawn aside in the huge tennis hall. The choir was singing and the stage was set. For a moment there was an awed silence and then suddenly a burst of applause as people gazed at what was a veritable Paradise. A great domed hemisphere of deep blue represented the heavens. Stars sparkled brightly and the planets moved in orbit propelled by cleverly concealed machinery. On one side rose Mount Olympus, home of the Greek gods, its peak reaching the blue heavens. Down from the mountain gods and goddesses floated miraculously. Leonardo had outdone himself. This Paradise Festival was talked of for many years.

To celebrate the gift of a sacred relic, a nail from the True Cross, Duke Lodovico decided to hold a religious festival in the great Cathedral. He engaged Leonardo to work out the mechanics of displaying it, high above the altar. Leonardo created a device of cleverly hidden ropes and pulleys. On the day of this celebration, known as the Feast of the Holy Nail, the Cathedral was full to overflowing. While the choir sang, the sacred nail, encased in a lovely crystal and gilt casket embedded in an enormous iron cross, rose up slowly and mysteriously, no machinery being visible. The precious relic came to rest in a niche above the high altar. There, spotlighted by flaming lamps, it could be seen by all. The multitude fell on its knees. "Alleluia, alleluia," the chant rose and fell. The sacred relic in its casket can still be seen in Milan's Cathedral where it is lowered once a year for the populace to venerate.

It was such feats as these that first made Leonardo famous in Milan. But finally the duke made use of Leonardo's ability as an artist. He was commissioned to make a bronze statue of Lodovico's father, Francesco Sforza, first duke of the house of Sforza to rule Milan. Leonardo then became Lodovico's official court artist and set up his studio in the ducal palace. He decided to make his figure of Francesco on horseback to emphasize his warriorlike and powerful character.

Leonardo visited the duke's stables and sketched horses in all sorts of poses. He studied their anatomy carefully before he made a model for the final statue. He has left us many excellent drawings of horses, showing them in spirited action or majestic repose. One of the early designs for this huge statue shows the horse rearing. But Leonardo soon realized that such a pose for a statue of the size he planned was not feasible. He decided on a statelier, slow-paced horse with a dignified and authoritative rider keeping it in check.

He soon set to work on the large clay model. As usual with Leonardo, it took him a long time to complete the statue, almost ten years. He did not work on it constantly, but often abandoned it to pursue a more pressing interest.

Early sketch of horse and rider for the Sforza Monument.

ROYAL COLLECTION, WINDSOR CASTLE

When the great clay model, from which the bronze statue would finally be cast, was finished, it was a wonder to behold. Rising to a height of twenty-six feet, the horse reined in, the rider erect in his seat, it was a majestic piece of work, the very symbol of power and strength that Lodovico wanted. The duke in his impatience to show it off had the large clay model wheeled to the gateway of his palace. The Emperor Maximilian was arriving in Milan to marry the duke's niece, Bianca. With what greater piece of art could Milan impress the emperor? The people were astounded by its size and splendor—and its lifelike quality. News of this great statue, the Colossus as it was called, spread rapidly and Leonardo became famous overnight. It was sometimes referred to as the eighth wonder of the world.

But there was a sad ending to this wonder of the world. Fifty tons of bronze were needed to cast it in its final, permanent form. Duke Lodovico was involved in one of his petty wars with rival cities and felt it more important to use the bronze for cannon—the great horse could wait. And so it stayed in its clay, unprotected and exposed to the elements. The final tragedy came in 1499 when the French, under King Louis XII, captured Milan. French bowmen used the statue as a practice target and managed to sever its head and to break off many pieces. This work of art which represented almost ten years of labor was ruined in one moment of childish sport. Leonardo was heartbroken.

Perhaps the most famous Renaissance painting is *The Last Supper*. Leonardo was commissioned to do a wall painting in the duke's favorite church, the Santa Maria delle Grazie. The painting was to be on an end wall of the monks' refectory or dining hall. Before Leonardo started on this work, which was to take several years, he made careful studies for it. Until this time most wall paintings had been done in fresco (painting with dry paint on wet plaster), which meant that the artist had to work fast and finish his painting before the plaster dried. He could not change things once they were painted. Leonardo decided to use tempera (pigments mixed with egg yolk) on a dry wall primed with chalk and glue instead of on a plain wet surface. He could work as slowly and carefully as he wanted and his wall priming would make his painting last.

The job assigned was a difficult one, to paint Christ and his twelve disciples at their last meal together. Leonardo thought about this painting day and night. He chose a dramatic moment to portray, the moment when Christ said that one of his disciples would betray him. Leonardo searched everywhere for the right faces to serve as models. He painted the faces with the utmost care, each seeming to reveal his inmost thoughts. "Is it I?" each face seems to say. He arranged the twelve disciples in groups of three with the calm, still figure of Christ in the center. The two faces which caused Leonardo the most trouble were those of Jesus, the Christ, and Judas, the betrayer. To find features worthy of the Christ and base enough for Judas gave him countless hours of worry and searching.

Duke Lodovico and the monks became impatient. Sometimes the artist would paint feverishly all day and far into the night, never stopping to eat. Then he would abandon his work for days at a time. When questioned by the duke, Leonardo replied that one often worked hardest when one appeared to work least, that the thinking about how to paint a picture was as important as the painting of it. And so Leonardo took his time thinking, searching for models, and painting. He went to the worst areas of the city, watched the faces of criminals and the scum of humanity to find a perfect Judas. The completed face of Judas is in deep shadow in contrast to the other apostles. It has an evil expression. Unable to create to his satisfaction the perfect face of Jesus, he left it somewhat unfinished and yet it emanates a spiritual calm in contrast to the questioning faces of his disciples. A distinguished Italian wrote, "How amazing is the accuracy with which the apostles have been glimpsed at that very moment when the divine voice utters the terrible truth: 'One of you will betray me!' "

This seemed the climax of all that art had been striving for since the early Renaissance painters first tried to break away from the flat and unreal medieval way of painting. Not only was this a masterpiece to stir one's soul, it was also a masterpiece of geometrical design and perspective. All the details, such as the cut fish on the plate, the salt which has been knocked over by Judas, the glass half full of transparent wine, all these humble details help make this dramatic scene come to life. How men must have marveled at this masterpiece when the paint was fresh and the colors bright!

Like the equestrian statue, *The Last Supper* caused widespread amazement and admiration. Painters flocked to see it, pilgrims came to worship at it. Never had a single painting caused such a stir.

The Last Supper by Leonardo.

ALINARI PHOTO

Artists begged Leonardo to explain his methods so that they could learn from him. "The most important consideration in painting is that the movement of each figure express its mental state, such as desire, scorn, pity, and the like. People ought not to copy other painters' works but study nature," he said. "Painting," he advised, "is concerned with all attributes of sight, darkness, brightness, substance and color, form and place, remoteness and nearness, movement and rest." He pointed out the use of light and shade and urged artists to note even the unimportant details of nature. Even in *The Last Supper,* through the windows, beyond the arresting group of men and Jesus, is a quiet countryside of sky, hills, and streams.

Again tragedy was to beset Leonardo. Even in his lifetime the tempera which he had applied to such a carefully prepared wall began to flake and fall off. In spite of attempts to preserve it, it was not until recent times that its disintegration was known to be caused by dampness. It is now properly cared for and miraculously escaped a bombing in World War II which damaged the roof and a side wall of the refectory. Though it has lost its original perfection, *The Last Supper* still casts a spell of wonder and admiration.

But before Leonardo knew the sad fate of his painting he had left Milan, for when the French King Louis XII captured the city, he sent Duke Lodovico as a prisoner to France. Without his patron and with Milan in confusion, Leonardo decided to return to Florence, the city of his youth.

Mona Lisa by Leonardo.

ALINARI PHOTO

Florence had changed since his absence of seventeen years and was, like Milan, in a state of war. Maybe because of war all around him, but more probably because of his interest in mechanics, Leonardo now spent much time designing war machines. But at the same time he also painted his lovely *St. Anne and the Virgin and the Infant Jesus* and began work on his famous portrait, *Mona Lisa.* This painting, which now hangs in the Louvre in Paris, has intrigued people for centuries. It is not that the face is so beautiful but that the smile and expression are so arresting. One wants to know what this woman is thinking about and what her strange half-smile means. Is it a happy smile or a sad smile, or a smile of scorn and disdain? Whatever the smile may mean, this portrait stirs the imagination. Set against a strange background of misty mountains, rocks, and streams, Mona Lisa keeps her thoughts to herself.

It seems odd that an artist who could paint such sublime pictures could also be interested in designing implements of warfare. Leonardo did not like war, for he was far too gentle, kind, and wise. But the fascination of invention seemed to overcome any thought he had about war's horror and stupidity. In any case he did design all kinds of war machines and was even employed by Cesare Borgia, a man whose very life was war and violence.

Cesare Borgia was a dashing young courtier, full of ideas of intrigue and eager for power. He wanted to conquer all of Italy. He must have heard of Leonardo's many talents, for he hired him not as an artist but as a military engineer.

In 1502, when Leonardo joined the power-seeking prince, Borgia was already hated and feared for his cruel and ruthless ways. But the Florentine Machiavelli admired him so much that he wrote a book, *The Prince,* in praise of Borgia's power politics.

Leonardo followed this prince from city to city, advising and planning war machines and methods for attacks and sieges.

There is no proof that any of Leonardo's military inventions were actually made and used. He has, however, left us many sketches and descriptions of his different types of machines. He invented armored tanks. "These will take the place of elephants—it will take eight men to work and make it turn and pursue the enemy. This is good to break through the enemy but it must be followed up." He devised chariots with revolving scythes on a projecting shaft and with sharp cutters jutting from the wheels; "these

Sketches of scything machine and tanks by Leonardo.

TRUSTEES OF THE BRITISH MUSEUM

will mow down men like a field of grain." He invented a machine with a revolving platform for discharging a succession of arrows. He even had plans for diving suits and submarines. But he gave no detailed account of the submarine because of "the evil nature of man" and his fear of the destruction it would cause. He may have thought that many of his machines were too deadly for mankind. Of course most of Leonardo's inventions, from machine guns to submarines, have been built in our own time.

While working for Cesare Borgia, Leonardo not only devised war machines, he also helped in such engineering projects as draining swamps, improving canals and irrigation systems. He made excellent topographical maps.

Cesare Borgia was brilliantly successful in capturing many Italian city-states. But when a new Pope, Julius II, was elected, his one idea was to get rid of this powerful young prince. He managed to capture Cesare and send him off to prison in Spain. Cesare Borgia's fall from power and glory was even more rapid than his rise.

Once again Leonardo was without an employer and once again he returned to the city of his youth, Florence. Whether he was finally disgusted with Cesare's war enterprises we do not know. But when Leonardo was commissioned to paint the victorious battle of the Florentines at Anghiari, Leonardo depicted a scene of horror, not a noble victory. He showed what he felt about war, that it was "bestial frenzy," anything but glorious. He depicted warriors contorted in fear and cruelty, horses writhing and rearing in agony. It was a scene of death and destruction.

And he now gave up war inventions and turned his attention to something that had fascinated him for a long time, the flight of birds. Leonardo often bought caged birds just to set them free. He happily watched them wing their way to freedom. He studied in detail just what makes birds stay aloft, how the flapping of their wings propels them upward, and how they glide on a current of air; how they slow down for landing by spreading their feathers and lowering their tails. He observed their steering methods, one wing lowered, the tail used as a rudder. He studied not only the flight of birds but also other winged creatures—bats, dragonflies, and butterflies. They beat their wings downward to rise up, backward to go forward, and spread their wings and dipped their tails to land—why couldn't man devise a way to do this? Could not such a strong animal as man manipulate wings—if wings could be created for him? Leonardo figured that wings for a man should be about sixty feet across and that they should imitate "no other than the bat's."

And so he set to work to construct a flying machine with wings built on the principle of a bat's, of leather bound by strong silken cords. The body was a sort of seat for a man, whose torso would control the movement of the wings. A tail-shaped rudder was attached by cords to the neck and controlled by movements of the head. There is a mountain near Florence where Leonardo planned to try out his great flying machine and there were rumors that people did see a huge, strange bird take off from the mountain.

One of Leonardo's pupils appeared with a broken leg. People wondered if he had been "the bird."

Our only evidence of his flying machine, or machines, is in his notebooks where one can read of his plans and see his drawings. If his flying machine was ever tried, it was surely a failure and another disappointment for Leonardo. He also had plans for an enormous "aerial screw," a sort of helicopter device with revolving wings. And thinking of the dangers of flight, he devised a parachute. "If man have a tent of linen with no openings and it be twenty feet across and twenty-four feet deep he can throw himself down from any height without injury."

It is sad but not surprising that after so many years of careful study and experimenting Leonardo did not create a successful flying machine. But, as if looking into the future, he was convinced that one day man would conquer the air. His studies of currents of air and winds, the gliding and flight of birds, helped man in his gropings toward his final conquest of the air.

After Leonardo's last great painting, the *Mona Lisa,* he became more and more interested in science. Searching for jobs, he wandered back to Milan and was employed by the French for a few years. Then in hopes that the new Pope, Leo X, son of Lorenzo de' Medici, would give him work, he set off to Rome at the age of sixty, but he found that younger men, Michelangelo and Raphael, had all the important commissions. Pope Leo grew impatient with Leonardo's slowness and his strange interests, for Leonardo spent much of his time in Rome at the hospitals, studying anatomy. He dissected human bodies, studied muscles, bones, and the circulation of blood. He almost but not quite understood the circulatory system, how the heart and its blood vessels worked.

In the Middle Ages dissecting human bodies had been forbidden by the Church. In the Renaissance it was still frowned upon by some churchmen but it was being more and more accepted as man became more and more interested in himself. Leonardo was not the only curious scientist who dissected bodies—there were many others, but Leonardo understood far more than the others.

He was first interested in anatomy for the sake of his painting.

Leonardo's sketches of flight machine, aerial screw, and parachute, and modern models made from them.

INTERNATIONAL BUSINESS MACHINES CORPORATION

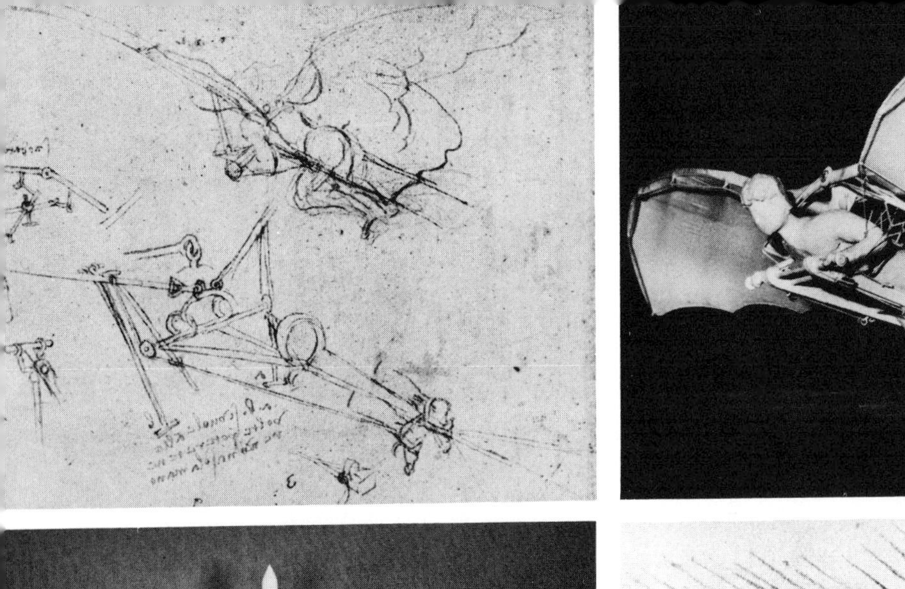

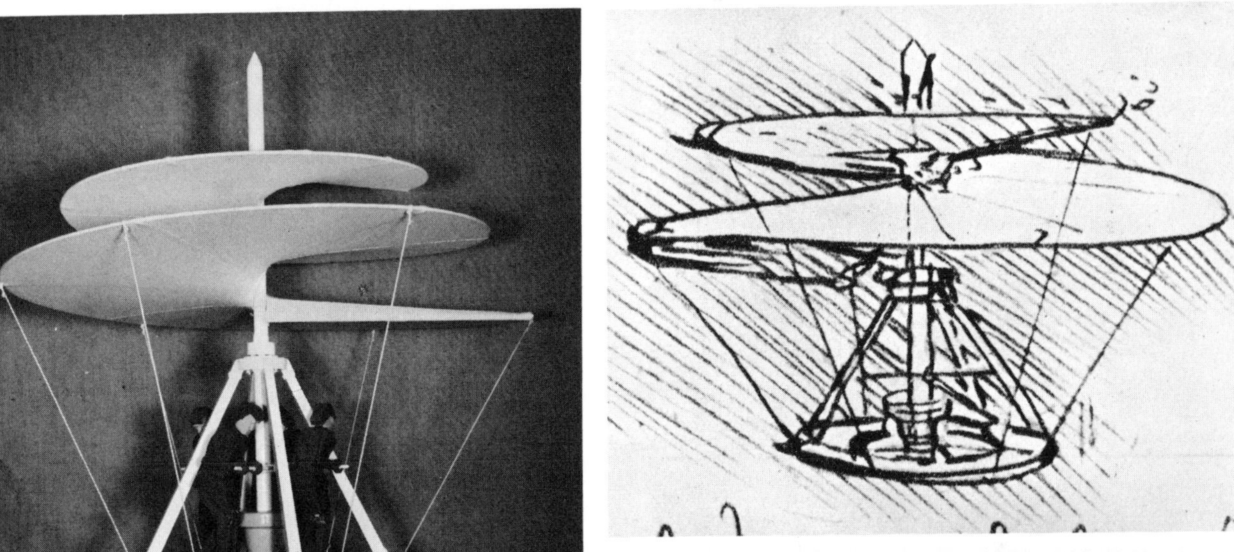

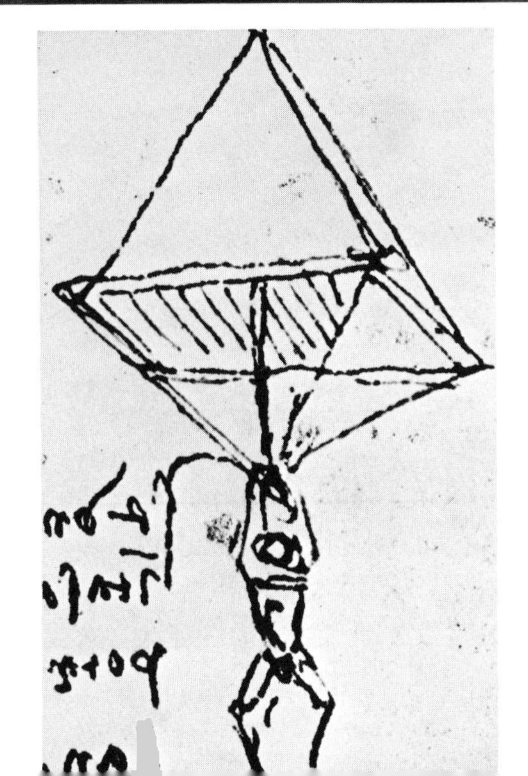

He wanted to know the exact construction of the human body in every detail before he painted it. But he became so absorbed in how the body functions that the study of anatomy for its own sake became a passion with him. His careful and detailed drawings of the body and its various organs are not only works of art but so accurate that they are still valuable for medical research.

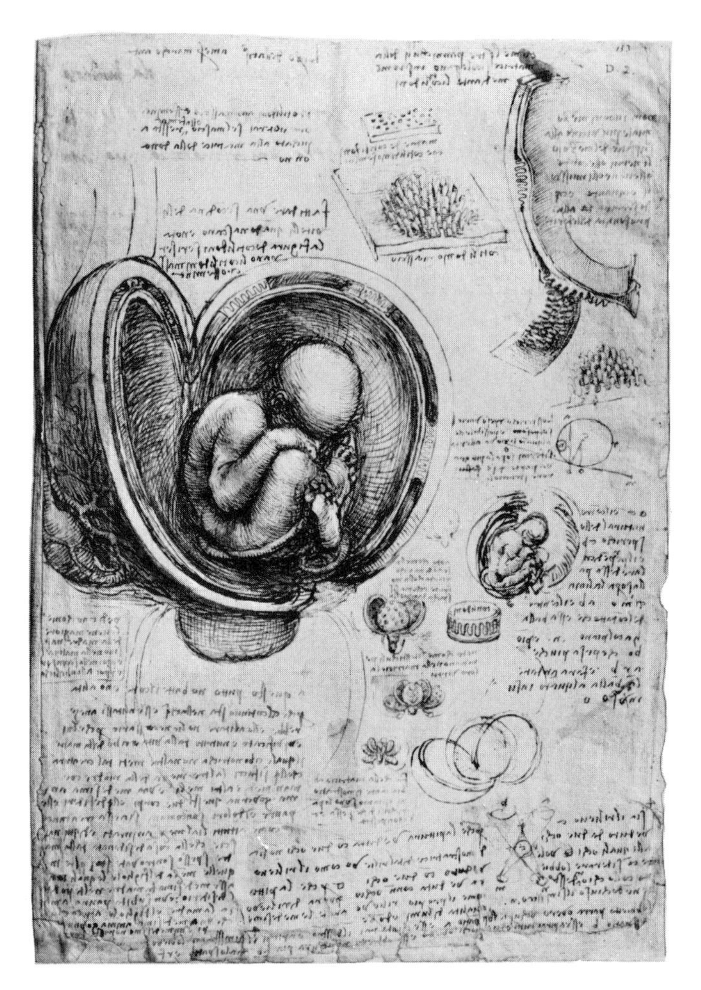

Anatomical drawing of foetus by Leonardo.

ROYAL COLLECTION, WINDSOR CASTLE

The city of Milan, which had been going through many upheavals since Duke Lodovico's capture, was still a haven for Leonardo. Knowing he was not wanted or needed in Rome, he set off once more for Milan which the new young King of France, Francis I, was now occupying. Full of enthusiasm for Italian art and learning, the king eagerly invited Leonardo to go back with him to France, as court painter.

Leonardo was an old man when he said farewell to Italy. Even so he had to help with pageants and masked balls at the gay and sumptuous court of Francis I. For one festive occasion he made a mechanical lion which walked across the stage and stopped before the king. When tapped by the royal sword, the lion reared up and opened his chest. From its deep blue interior fell masses of lilies, the flowers of France. But King Francis also appreciated Leonardo's greater talents, saying that "never had anyone come into the world who knew so much—not only in sculpture, painting, and architecture, for in addition he was also a great philosopher."

Leonardo's achievements in painting—his perfection of the art of perspective, his use of light and shade, and his ability to depict not only a likeness in a face but the very soul behind it—are enough to mark him as a genius among painters of his time. That he was also a pioneer in scientific experiments, an inventor, and a philosopher marks the extraordinary breadth of his genius. When we think of Renaissance man with his many interests and many accomplishments, we think of Leonardo da Vinci. But Leonardo was more than a typical Renaissance man for his unusual creativity in so many fields has never been equaled. He was an artist in search of beauty and a scientist in search of truth.

His own words would have been fitting at his deathbed: "As a day well spent makes it sweet to sleep, so a life well used makes it sweet to die."

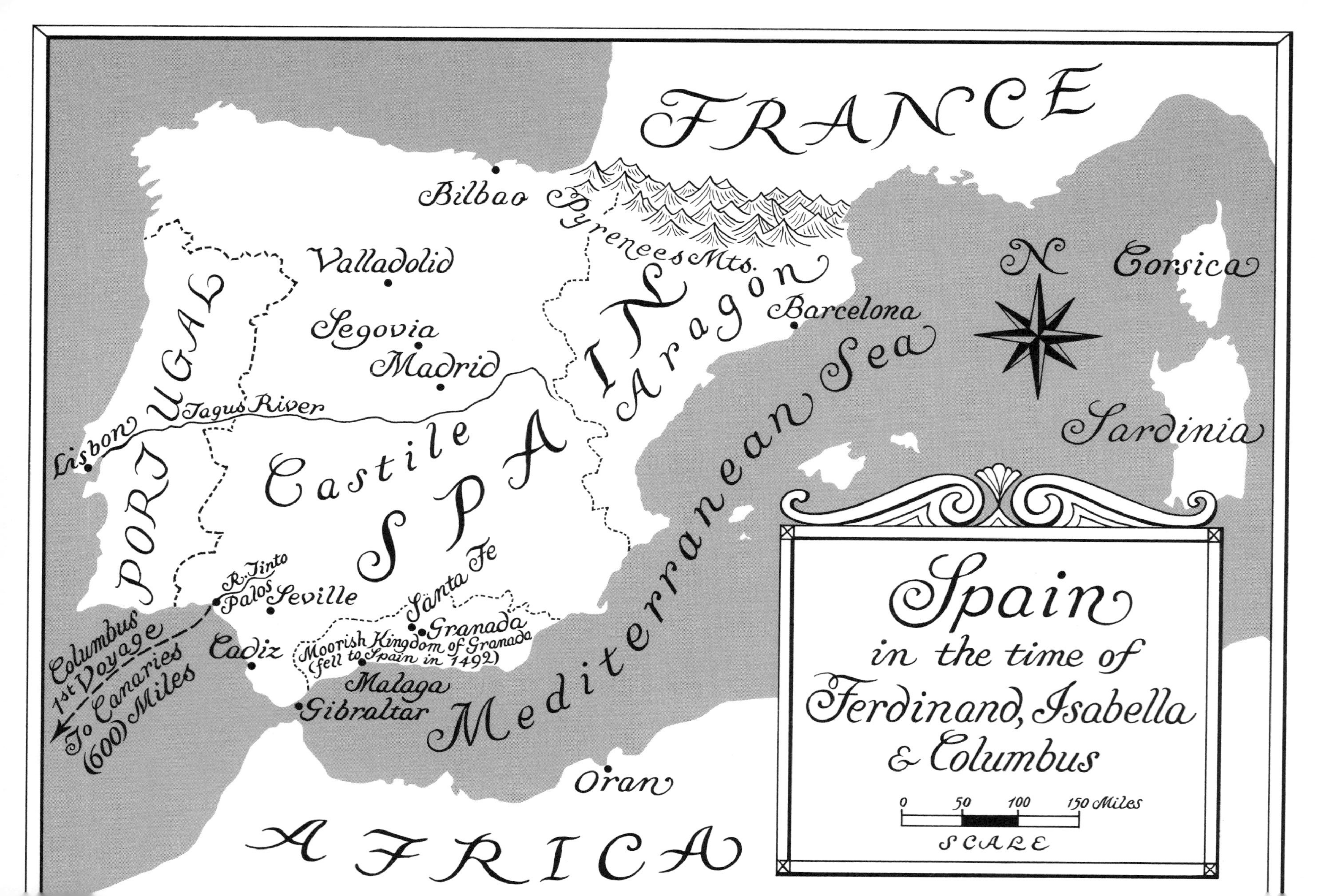
FRANCE
Bilbao
Pyrenees Mts.
Valladolid
Segovia
Madrid
Corsica
Sardinia
N
Barcelona
Aragon
SPAIN
PORTUGAL
Tagus River
Lisbon
Castile
R. Tinto
Palos
Seville
Santa Fe
Granada
Moorish Kingdom of Granada
(fell to Spain in 1492)
Cadiz
Malaga
Gibraltar
Mediterranean Sea
Columbus 1st Voyage
To Canaries
(600) Miles
Oran
AFRICA
Spain
in the time of
Ferdinand, Isabella
& Columbus
0
50
100
150 Miles
SCALE

PART 2
SPAIN AWAKES

A shepherd on the central highlands of Spain.

SPANISH NATIONAL TOURIST OFFICE

WHILE the Italy of Lorenzo and Leonardo remained disunited and divided, Spain was evolving in another way. The Renaissance, with its new ideas and enthusiasms, took a different form there. During these exciting new times Spain's little states united under a central, powerful monarchy. With a surge of nationalistic feeling, Spain shook off centuries of isolation and small civil wars. Within a single generation she became a great empire.

Spain is a harsher land than Italy. At its northernmost part are the forbidding Pyrenees Mountains, cutting off the Spanish people from easy contact with the rest of Europe. Its central provinces are mostly of high tableland, sparse and rugged, broken by rocky, treeless hills. Dry winds sweep over this yellow-brown area most of the year; only in the rainy seasons can wheat be raised here. It is so harsh a plateau that the ancient Romans said that a nightingale trying to cross it would have to take its food and drink along. Most of Spain's rivers are canyon rivers, wild and full of waterfalls, drying up in the hot summers and not good for shipping at any time. But parts of Spain are green: the forests and misty coastal regions of the north, with meadows and pastures for raising cattle, and the terraced hills of the eastern provinces where oranges and lemons and grapes grow in profusion. Parts of the subtropical southern land have been irrigated for hundreds of years; sugar cane and date palms and olive groves interrupt the scorched landscape.

Spain has the good luck to face two great bodies of water—the Mediterranean Sea and the Atlantic Ocean—and this, of course, has had great effect upon its history. It also faces Africa, separated at its closest tip by less than ten miles; and this too has given it a different history from the rest of Europe.

The straits that separate Spain from Africa were called the Pillars of Hercules by the ancient Greeks. To them, and to most of the ancient Mediterranean people, the Pillars marked the boundaries of their world. The dark Atlantic Ocean beyond and the tales of the wild tribes on the western Spanish coast frightened mariners. Rumors spread of sea monsters and terrible storms.

When the Roman Empire took over the Mediterranean world, the native Spanish tribes put up a hard fight but were finally conquered. Gradually the Romans civilized the tribes, and Spain became their favored province. Spain's grainfields fed the great Roman armies. Its coastal cities grew in splendor, full of fine arenas and marble bathing houses and temples. Seven Spaniards even succeeded in becoming Roman emperors. Cadiz, on the western coast of Spain, became the second largest city in the Roman Empire.

Then, as had happened in Italy, the northern barbarians swept into Spain in the fifth century. One tribe in particular, the Visigoths, remained there. At first they massacred the people and destroyed the fine roads and buildings left by the Romans, but gradually the barbarians settled down peacefully with the Spanish inhabitants. The culture of the Spanish people, influenced so long by Rome, rubbed some of the barbarian roughness away. In time barbarian and Spaniard became one people, speaking a sort of Spanish Latin and worshiping in Christian churches. The Visigothic kings of Spain were Christian kings. They built Christian churches and monasteries. Visigothic bishops traveled to Rome to see their spiritual head, the Pope. Spain was peaceful and fruitful once more.

But again an invasion took place. Moorish armies crossed over from Africa in A.D. 711, and Mohammedan pushed Christian far back into the mountains of the north. Their backs to the wall of the Pyrenees, the Spanish Christians could retreat no farther. In their bleak and damp fortresses they watched with envy the Moorish kingdom flourish in southern Spain, with its beautiful mosques, palaces, and cleverly irrigated fields which produced cotton and silkworms to make fine cloth, and fat sheep for the profitable Mediterranean woolen trade. The immense wealth and culture of the Moors in Spain were far superior to the rough and poor life of the northern Christians, then in the very depths of the Dark Ages.

For hundreds of years Spanish Christian battled Spanish Moor. Over three thousand heroic battles were fought as the tough men from the northern mountains gradually pushed the Moslem enemy southward. The Spanish feudal knights of the frontier wore iron crucifixes next to their skin. Churchmen rode with them into battle, and religious fervor drove them on to victory after victory. Finally, in the thirteenth century, a single enemy area remained in southeastern Spain—the rich kingdom of Granada. For two hundred years not a dent was made in the well-fortified, mountainous boundaries of this Moorish kingdom.

By the fifteenth century most of the feudal states of Christian Spain had gradually combined into two chief kingdoms, Aragon and Castile. Aragon, to the east, faced the important Mediterranean seacoast with good harbors and ports. Castile was the larger of the two, touching the Atlantic to the north and south. Castile means castle—its lands were dotted with hundreds of them, owned by tough medieval lords and churchmen. Both Castile and Aragon wanted to drive the Moors away from their southern borders and out of Spain altogether. But, typical of feudal countries everywhere, they would not combine their strength. Such a combination would be needed to drive the ancestral enemy from this rich, important part of Spanish land.

Fortunately at the end of the fifteenth century two great rulers, Ferdinand of Aragon and Isabella of Castile, welded their two countries into a united Spain. Guided by their new concepts of power and expansion, Spain changed from a typical medieval country into a successful, imperialistic Renaissance nation.

The castle in Segovia where Isabella was living when she became queen.

SPANISH NATIONAL TOURIST OFFICE

FERDINAND AND ISABELLA

Ferdinand and Isabella of Spain.

In Renaissance times emerged the all-powerful monarch who ruthlessly took away the power of competing nobles and stubbornly resisted the efforts of the church to tell him what to do. This Renaissance monarch made national laws and saw that they were enforced. He made deals and treaties with other monarchs, gambling with the fate of his nation as if it were a private toy. Parliaments and courts and armies did not control him—he controlled them.

King Ferdinand and Queen Isabella were spectacular examples of this new type of monarch. Together they took the ineffective little kingdoms of Castile and Aragon and made them into a giant nation, Spain, free of internal enemies, with an overseas empire larger than even the ancient Romans ever had. It was not an easy task, but both had the courage and determination to carry them successfully over every hurdle.

Ferdinand was born in 1452 in Aragon, the mountainous eastern kingdom in Spain with its long coast line on the Mediterranean. His boyhood was tough and hard, for at a very early age he gave up any schooling to follow his father from battlefield to battlefield. His clever and ferocious father, the King of Aragon, gave Ferdinand fine training for the future, for he spent his whole life fighting treacherous nobles, subduing restless provinces, and bargaining to keep his power.

Princess Isabella meanwhile was leading a different life in the bigger Spanish kingdom, Castile. She spent much of her lonely girlhood in a little town away from the luxurious life of her brother, King Henry—reading, embroidering, and studying under the guidance of the priests of the household and her devout mother.

Princess Isabella.

But like young Ferdinand over the border, she too had to learn to live through intrigue and danger. Many people, tired of the court's behavior, were attracted by her simplicity of dress, her piety, and her dignified and pleasing manner. Ambitious nobles, diplomats from far lands, and powerful churchmen tried to make deals with her rather than with the king. He became jealous and suspicious of her popularity, for he was very unpopular and his foolish and extravagant rule was ruining the country. He surrounded Isabella with his spies. She had to be tactful and endlessly patient, and to bide her time cleverly.

The King of Castile tried to marry her to someone of no importance, but he was foiled by the clever king of neighboring Aragon, who had long planned to have her marry his son. He sent emissaries to Isabella, singing the praises of young Ferdinand. The princess was soon persuaded. She sent Prince Ferdinand a secret message asking him to join her quickly before her brother could interfere. Ferdinand, disguised as a stableboy, had to make his way over the mountainous borderland in order to avoid patrols sent by the king of Castile to ambush him. Finally he arrived at the friendly Castilian town of Valladolid where nobles welcomed him and paid homage to him. There he met Isabella for the first time.

He saw a lovely young girl of eighteen with bright blue eyes and fresh, glowing skin. Her auburn hair shone beneath a simple headdress. Her modesty made her quiet and reserved, but she held herself with great dignity. She spoke to him in the most elegant and polished Castilian—the purest of the many Spanish dialects of the day.

At this time Ferdinand was seventeen years old, muscular and tanned from his years in the army. He had flowing chestnut hair, a finely shaped nose and mouth, and unusually white teeth. In spite of little schooling, and a boyhood spent with rough soldiers, he had a courteous and agreeable manner. Already he had a reputation for courage and prudence.

Everyone at this historic meeting was overjoyed and full of hope for the future. The many Castilian nobles present were more anxious than ever to give their allegiance to this attractive pair rather than to the foolish, weak King Henry.

Plans for the wedding were quickly made, and after one more meeting the prince and the princess were married, on October 19, 1469. Ferdinand's purse had been stolen on the way to the wedding, and Isabella did not have much of an allowance from her jealous brother. Both were so poor that they had to borrow money to pay for the ceremony.

Young King Ferdinand in armor.

King Henry of Castile received the news of this forbidden marriage with rage. Every day more of his nobles deserted him to join this wise young couple. It was obvious to all that Isabella was concerned about the terrible condition of the Castilian people, so impoverished by the king's foolish rule. When the king finally died in 1474 few missed him. With wild acclaim Isabella and Ferdinand were proclaimed joint rulers of Castile in a splendid ceremony and glorious procession in the old city of Segovia. The unsheathed sword of state was carried on high, banners waved in the winter winds, and guns and bells made a loud and joyful noise. With true humility Isabella threw herself before the golden altar of the cathedral and gave thanks to God for His protection, imploring Him also to guide her in the coming difficulties of her task. Grandees, churchmen, and governors from all parts of the country kissed her hand and swore oaths of allegiance to the royal pair.

At last, after centuries of separation, the crowns of Aragon and Castile were united. The way lay open to future greatness.

The young rulers faced enormous difficulties. The fierce Moors held a prosperous piece of southern Spain, and though Ferdinand and Isabella longed to chase them out, they had neither the money nor the army to do so. The country had been weakened by years of fighting. For too long, powerful nobles, uncontrolled by weak kings, had made a wilderness of former wheatfields, olive groves, and pastures. Peasants, not knowing where to turn as they saw their grain and sheep stolen by bands of soldiers, had taken to robbing travelers on lonely, unprotected roads. Robber knights in high stone fortresses overlooking caravan routes became rich and went unpunished. Travel from one town to another became too risky, so the roads were gradually deserted and overgrown with grasses and scrub.

The first thing the two sovereigns had to do was to bring peace to their countryside. First they organized a national police force to keep order in the land. Every town had to pay for part of this force. Ferocious penalties were handed out: a wrongdoer had an ear, hand, or leg cut off—or was hanged. Rich wrongdoers were punished as well as the poor.

One wealthy knight offered an enormous amount of gold to have his death sentence revoked, but though the kingdom needed money the sovereigns did not relent. They knew what effective examples these severe penalties would be to other rebellious nobles. In a few years the bandits and robber chieftains were wiped out.

More disagreeable surprises were in store for the nobility. They had to return money and property which had been granted to them by earlier, more careless kings. Many of their castles were demolished by the sovereigns, who forbade them to build new ones. In a single province fifty fortresses, the strongholds of robber knights, were razed. When certain grandees objected furiously to these measures, Isabella became just as furious that they should dare to question her authority, and told them firmly that she and Ferdinand had no intention of becoming tools in their hands.

The king and queen then saw to it that offices—even the smallest—were held by people of merit, such as lawyers and teachers, often of humble birth. Formerly only rich or noble people had held positions of importance. The sovereigns picked judges of fairness and integrity, and often presided themselves at the courts of justice, seeing that everyone, great or small, got a fair sentence. People watching the king and queen perform these duties so zealously proclaimed that an Age of Justice had arrived.

Isabella turned her attention to some of the powerful clergy who owned rich abbeys, convents, and even whole towns. Soon only honest, pious, and learned churchmen got the highest positions. The queen then bravely tackled another problem. Many vast church lands had been assigned by the Pope to foreign churchmen who never came to Spain but collected revenues just the same. Isabella took these lands away from the foreigners. The Pope in a rage sent word that he did not have to consult any potentate on earth about church appointments, but Isabella stood firm. Devout though she was, there was never any question in her mind that the welfare of her country came first.

The royal authority was now supreme. The lives of the two sovereigns were a fine example to their people. Both had great dignity and energy. Both lived very simply and economically, scorning to spend the kingdom's money on feasting, dress, and show.

Isabella and Ferdinand traveled over their kingdom for the greater part of every year. Nothing escaped their observant eyes.

Their whole court—soldiers, priests, magistrates, attendants—would accompany them by litter, on mule or horseback.

In order to keep a better eye on the nobles and their families, Ferdinand and Isabella invited them to leave their remote provinces and join them at court, bringing their children with them to be educated with the young Crown Prince Juan and the four princesses. In this way the young nobles would not grow up frivolous and ignorant of everything except war, but instead would have the best education that the court could provide.

Isabella was determined that her children should have a better education than hers and Ferdinand's. Though rather an old-fashioned person in many ways, she was curious about the new learning then moving slowly from Italy to other European states. Realizing that Spain had been backward, she summoned men of the Italian Renaissance to her court. Italian tutors were put in charge of the education of the royal children. The latest Italian sculpture and tapestries were imported; and more than two hundred Renaissance paintings were collected by the queen to hang on high palace walls. The children were taught Latin poetry and Greek philosophy. The crown prince, Ferdinand's and Isabella's only son, had a separate court and school of his own, with ten young nobles selected as his constant companions in study and play.

Isabella herself took up the study of Latin. The new learning became fashionable under her patronage. Thanks to her example, Spanish women took an unusual share in the new studies. The queen's Latin teacher was a woman. Other women even lectured at the great Spanish universities.

The princesses were as well educated as if they had been men. In addition to customary accomplishments such as playing musical instruments and sewing, they were taught to read and speak Latin as fluently as if it had been their native tongue. There were no better educated young ladies in all of Europe. Their father and mother, already planning their future marriages to kings, knew that Renaissance queens should not be outshone in their accomplishments by anyone.

Eminent scholars from other countries flocked to Spain, for they

Renaissance palace at Salamanca, decorated by stone scallop-shells, emblems of the patron saint of Spain, Saint James.

SHELL OIL COMPANY

were sure of a welcome from the queen. Spanish scholars were also encouraged by the queen to study in Italy. Before her rule there had been few schools in the kingdom; now universities, endowed by Isabella, sprang up in many cities.

One can see today in a museum Isabella's own collection of books and manuscripts, some well worn by her eager hands. When the new Renaissance invention of printing was introduced into Spain, Isabella immediately saw its great advantage in the spreading of knowledge. She ordered many books to be printed at her expense, and helped printers establish themselves in the cities of the realm.

All over Spain buildings with a new look began to rise, as Italian architects added their ideas to the native Spanish style. Although Ferdinand and Isabella loved to economize, they also loved to build. They employed the most skillful carvers and stonemasons. Buildings were decorated lavishly with lacy grillwork and complicated arches and balconies. Sometimes the fronts of houses would be studded with carved stones. In the southern parts of Spain the idea of the Moorish patio was borrowed for the new Spanish palaces and town houses. A whole style of Spanish architecture, combining the ideas of the Italian Renaissance with Moorish and Spanish styles, is called "Isabelline" after the great Spanish queen. This architectural style can be seen today in the South American countries and in the southwestern United States.

The land began to prosper again. Roads were repaired, and more than seven hundred new bridges spanned the deep canyon rivers. Foreign trade improved. Bowstaves and fine iron and leather were sent to England. Velvets from Toledo, honey and sweet oils, dried fruits such as figs and dates and raisins from the southern districts were exported everywhere. In the north every year seven or eight thousand pack mules would trudge through scrub oak and heather carrying as many as fifteen thousand packs of famous Spanish wool to the northern port of Bilbao, where a fleet would carry the wool to the flourishing port of Antwerp. Fine wool was also shipped from the port of Barcelona, on the Mediterranean, to be woven into beautiful cloth in Florence and other Mediterranean cities.

But just as Spain's Renaissance was reaching an impressive height, the queen took a step which set back Spanish cultural progress. Isabella, counseled in her lonely girlhood by a fanatical monk called Torquemada, was obsessively devout. He had urged her, if she ever became queen, to wipe out all non-believers living in Spain. Although the Spanish people, like all Europeans, were mostly Catholic, there were in Spain two non-Catholic groups—the Mohammedan enemy in the south, and a small but important Jewish population. As the country grew stronger, the queen dreamed of driving out both of these heathen people for the glory of God and the Catholic faith. Normally she had the kindest of hearts and was quick to suffer for the misfortunes of others; but in matters of religion her heart was hard. As her armies were not yet strong enough to drive out the warlike Moors from southern Spain, she concentrated first on her country's other non-Christians, the Jews.

A victim of the Inquisition has had his hands chopped off, and is on a pulley so that his torture may be prolonged.

Under the terrible Inquisitor-General Torquemada, the Spanish Inquisition was set up to root out the Jewish heretics. It adopted grisly methods of spying, anonymous accusations, and torture. To the Inquisitors a rumor was reason enough to take a man's property away from him, imprison or maim him, or burn him at the stake. Pope Sixtus sanctioned Isabella's behavior, for he was glad to get his share of the money snatched from unfortunate Jewish families. Ferdinand, always on the lookout for income, also approved of the Inquisition. And most of the people of Spain took up the purge enthusiastically, for tolerance was a rare word in those days. It was easy for them to be jealous and resentful of the Jews, who through hard work and ambition had become the backbone of the middle classes—the scholars, doctors, bankers, and lawyers—in every Spanish town. Many had positions of trust at court, or managed vast estates for the nobility. Others ran the finances of the country, helping Spain to get on its feet again after years of feudal bankruptcy. Others loaned their gold to develop Spanish armies and equip Spanish caravels for trade and exploration.

Though many Jews had been converted to Christianity, there were many more who refused, and practiced their own religion in secret. So after about a dozen years, when the threats and terrors of the Inquisition did not seem to convince enough Jews that Christianity was better than the religion of their forefathers, the fanatical Isabella decided to banish all non-converted Jews from Spain unless they immediately accepted baptism. More than two hundred thousand chose to leave the land where they had lived for centuries. They had to sell their possessions for fractions of what they were worth—a house for a mule, a vineyard for a piece of cloth. Many starved in Africa or died from the plague on small, crowded boats sailing to other lands. Ferdinand would have preferred to let them stay in exchange for large fines for his treasury, but Isabella believed that God wanted Christian unity, even though Spain would lose the people who had contributed most to her wealth. Other civilized nations were shocked, yet many writers of the day celebrated the Christian enthusiasm of the Spanish queen. It seems strange that a system like the Inquisition, which closed its mind to freedom of inquiry, should have flourished at the same time that the light of the Renaissance was bringing new knowledge and civilization to Spain. Yet religious intolerance played a strong part in the life of the fifteenth century and other centuries to come.

As Ferdinand and Isabella became more powerful, and as the coffers of the royal treasury began to fill, they felt able to turn their attention to the other infidels in Spain—the Moors—trespassing for almost eight hundred years in the rich, well-fortified kingdom of Granada in the southeastern corner of Spain. Isabella wanted merely to wipe the faith of Islam from the face of the Spanish land.

A courtyard in the Alhambra, the Moorish palace in Granada.

SPANISH NATIONAL TOURIST OFFICE

Ferdinand was more realistic. He not only wanted to expand Spanish territory, but was tempted by the wealth which the conquest of Granada would bring.

Granada was indeed an enviable kingdom. Its climate was warm, its harbors deep. Years of careful irrigation by skillful Moorish farmers had made it a garden spot. The greatest city of this Moorish kingdom, also called Granada, was surrounded by a great wall with a thousand towers. The royal palace, called the Alhambra, on one of the red hills within the city walls, could hold forty thousand men. Its architecture was lacelike and colorful, with airy courtyards full of tall fountains and scented by spices and blossoms.

The Moors for centuries had been men of culture and taste, exceptional in astronomy, mathematics, and pharmacy. They had been tolerant of other faiths, allowing Christians and Jews to live in harmony among them—unlike the intolerant Christian kingdoms to the north. They were fine fighters, trained from childhood in the use of crossbow and sword.

The kings of Granada looked with contempt on the warring, ignorant Spaniards. They felt superior in every way and secure behind their wild mountains crested by great stone fortresses which no battering ram could destroy.

Fighting broke out on the border in 1482. Raid and counter-raid gradually grew into a full-scale war. Isabella was in her element, gathering supplies and men for the front. Ferdinand, yearning for glory, fought courageously and coolly in many battles.

It took the Spaniards ten years to drive out the Moors. Their policy was to fight in the balmy spring and fall; the winters were too cold and the summer too hot. Every summer when the army dispersed, thirty thousand foragers were employed to destroy Moorish farms and granaries. Spanish fleets meanwhile patrolled the sea, on the lookout for enemy supply ships from the Barbary Coast of Africa.

To pay for all this, the king and queen got the help of the Pope, who promised all sorts of advantages to those who contributed to the campaign. Isabella had no trouble borrowing other money, so deep was the people's confidence in her word. She was the soul of the war, riding through the ranks clad in complete mail. She set up hospitals for the sick and wounded and brought them clothes and money. She never allowed her commanders to relax. If they said that a Moorish town seemed too powerful to be taken by storm, she would collect additional fresh troops and more arms. No catastrophe would alter her unflinching purpose.

The Spanish army in the field glittered with gay pavilions, colored flags, and shining coats of arms. At night hundreds of torches glowed. Cavaliers were eager to show off before the sympathetic queen and the warlike king. In their bright armor they would challenge the Moorish knights to single combat on the wide fields below the Moorish walls. They galloped at each other with their long, unwieldy lances. Every rule of chivalry was observed by both sides. This custom from the old days of the Middle Ages survived longer in Spain than in other countries, for in the unusually long sieges of Moorish-held cities there was splendid opportunity for individual gallantry rather than army action. Cervantes, a famous Spanish author of the late sixteenth century, was thinking of these knightly encounters when he created Don Quixote, the mad old knight who challenged windmills and sheep to mortal combat.

But old-fashioned chivalry could never have knocked down the thick, high Moorish walls. One of the great inventions of the age of the Renaissance came to the aid of the Spaniards—cannon. The war of Granada revealed the power of artillery to the world. Although these cannon were heavy and clumsy, and made of pieces of iron bound together, they could throw balls of iron or marble weighing many hundreds of pounds against the Moorish walls. Foreign engineers showed the Spanish army commanders how to breach walls by exploding mines under them.

Spanish churchmen rode into battle under the flag of their patron St. James, carrying swords as well as crosses. The troops often imagined that they saw St. James himself on a milk-white horse, appearing in the clouds before a battle and holding up the cross to urge them on. With every Spanish victory a solemn and splendid procession would wind into the captured town. A huge cross would be raised high on the walls, the mosques would be sprinkled with holy water and turned into Christian churches with great singing and rejoicing.

The siege of Malaga.

The Moors battled desperately and valiantly, but their towns fell one by one to the Christian foe. In 1487 the Spaniards surrounded the important town of Malaga. Its inhabitants held out until they began to starve and had to eat vine leaves and cats and dogs. Disease and death struck many. From their battlements and housetops the Moors could see endless supplies of food and ammunition brought to the Spanish army by long streams of pack mules. Then, as a last straw, they saw King Ferdinand and Queen Isabella ride over the cloud-topped sierra to encourage the besiegers and review the battle lines. By the end of the year Malaga surrendered.

Ferdinand and Isabella punished the heroic population of the conquered town by making everyone, young and old, a slave. The king sent a present of a hundred young Moorish people to the Pope, and fifty young girls to the queen of Naples for her court; he handed the rest around as rewards to nobles and cavaliers.

By the ninth year of war every important city except the Moorish capital, Granada, had surrendered to Ferdinand and Isabella. Before this city the Spanish army appeared at last. Isabella in full armor rode in plain sight of enemy sentries. The dream of her life was soon to be realized.

A masterly stroke now discouraged the Moors completely: in front of the Moorish walls the Spaniards built a complete city of stone houses, stables for a thousand horses, and spacious avenues. This new city was called Santa Fe (Holy Faith). It was obvious to the besieged people that the Spanish army was prepared to stay there indefinitely. In despair they surrendered.

So the Moorish occupation of Spain came to an end. The Moorish king, Abdallah, left the city dejectedly at the head of fifty cavaliers. He paused to salute the impatient conquering sovereigns, then slowly rode to join his family in the mountains. At a rocky promontory he looked back on his lost city and burst into tears. One can climb these rocks today and imagine the scene; the place is called El Ultimo Sospiro del Moro (the Last Sigh of the Moor).

On the great red walls of the city appeared a huge silver cross, sparkling in the sun, while the flags of the sovereigns, instead of the Moorish crescent, waved from the towers of the Alhambra. The choir sang the Te Deum and the king and queen, the knights, the archers, the gunners and pikemen knelt to give thanks for the success of their ten-year crusade.

No feudal prince could have sustained such an effort. It took a new sort of nation and ruler to call up such a large army, pay for it, feed it, and keep it so long in the field.

The capitulation of Granada, with its splendid ceremonies, took place on January 2, 1492. Among the spellbound watchers kneeling in the winter sunlight was a tall, blue-eyed grizzled adventurer from Genoa named Christopher Columbus. That very year the King and Queen of Spain gave him three ships and sent him westward to find the Indies.*

His return to Spain in 1493 after his great voyage was the sensation of the age. His discovery of the New World changed the course of history. The Spanish sovereigns' gamble in financing his voyage was repaid a thousandfold, for Columbus handed Spain an overseas empire of unimagined size and wealth.

The sovereigns' first reaction to Columbus' success was delight that the Spanish had beaten their rival explorers, the Portuguese. They quickly tried to make sure that the Portuguese would not share in their discovery of a westward route to the Orient and applied to Pope Alexander VI for a dividing line between the Spanish and Portuguese territorial claims. Alexander was a Spaniard and in debt to Ferdinand and Isabella for his election. He was delighted to be called upon in such an important matter and issued a decree which drew an imaginary line from north to south, in the Atlantic Ocean, a hundred leagues west of the Portuguese-held islands of Cape Verde and the Azores. Anything to the west of this line, the Pope decreed, should belong to Spain. Having no idea that he was disposing of two huge continents, the Pope, swayed by the diplomacy of his two clever countrymen, gave away at a stroke of his pen a New World to the Spanish. Later the Portuguese protested so much that the Pope's line was pushed westward, and thus by another casual agreement the Portuguese were awarded Brazil, as yet unknown.

* See *Christopher Columbus,* page 86.

Ferdinand and Isabella and the ships of Columbus.

THE HISPANIC SOCIETY OF AMERICA

From the day of Columbus' return, Ferdinand and Isabella had an intelligent and practical curiosity about the New World. They wanted to know everything about it—its climate, soil, vegetables, inhabitants. In the years to come they encouraged settlers to go to the new colonies, giving them free passage and land. They sent out priests by the dozen to convert the Indians. At the expense of the government hundreds of farmers and builders and artisans left the mother country with livestock and grain and tools. Soon Spanish colonists had all their familiar Spanish food and animals and churches and houses far from home. Adventurers looked for gold in every river and hill. Indian slaves did all the heavy work, against the orders of Isabella, who proclaimed them freemen because they had been baptized Christians by the colonial priests. But she was too far away to enforce this rule. Ferdinand did not have the same strong feelings about Christian slaves, so long as their labor brought wealth to the colonies and Spain. Both sovereigns demanded an enormous percentage of any precious minerals or jewels that might be discovered.

Isabella kept up a steady interest in Columbus and the lands he discovered on subsequent voyages. But many years were to pass before his discoveries repaid the expenses of his expeditions. Ferdinand quickly lost interest in the affairs of the New World; though the glory was great, the returns were too meager. He let Isabella worry about the business of the Indies and the souls of the Indians, while he turned to matters dearer to his heart. His old kingdom, Aragon, looked inward on the Mediterranean, not outward to the Atlantic, and his first interest lay in European diplomacy. He wanted to make sure that the nations of Europe would not grow at the expense of Spain and he stopped at no deception to get his way.

First among Ferdinand's worries was the behavior of France. This kingdom to the north, the wealthiest and most populous in Europe, was growing like Spain into a modern, unified nation, and also was ambitious to follow the Renaissance trend of expansion and conquest. Ferdinand saw clearly that France was a dangerous rival to his own plans in the Mediterranean. As he cast covetous eyes on the southern half of Italy, he knew that the King of France was doing so too.

With its rich fields and luxurious cities full of treasures, Italy would be a great prize. There was no national feeling among the Italian states, as there was in Spain; since Lorenzo de' Medici's death, they were more divided and jealous of one another than ever. They would fall easily before the national army of either Spain or France.

Ferdinand formed secret plans to send Spanish armies to conquer the kingdom of Naples in Italy. As the French king made his own splendid invasion plans, he was careful to draw up a treaty of neutrality with Ferdinand. But no man was cleverer than Ferdinand in misinterpreting treaties if it served his country's purpose. The king of France was mortified to find, after marching down Italy unopposed to Naples, that Ferdinand's armies were to the south of him, using guerrilla tactics, trench warfare, and many of the new guns. Ferdinand also cleverly used the other weapon of modern diplomacy—international agreements against a common enemy. His diplomats and agents made a quick treaty with the Italian states and secretly stirred up discontent and rebellion against the French invader.

Within two years the French had to withdraw. The Spanish also withdrew, well satisfied with the turn of events. Ferdinand, because of his skillful use of allies, had spent little money. The French, on the other hand, had poured a large share of their wealth into this unsuccessful campaign. Ferdinand's international reputation as a wise and cautious monarch grew.

A few years later the French were determined to try again, and Ferdinand was again determined to outwit them. He sent a representative to the French to work out a peaceful division of Naples between them, but while this representative was being wined and dined by the French to celebrate this bloodless deal, the Spanish armies took all of Naples by force. Though the French called him perfidious, Ferdinand was unmoved by mere words. He had achieved his expansionist designs.

The Italian Machiavelli, who in 1513 wrote a famous book, *The Prince,* on how a ruler should achieve power, praised Ferdinand for his methods, calling him a new prince, whose actions were all very great, and some, extraordinary. The great monarchs of these expanding times gambled for vast territories and power. In this game Ferdinand was likely to emerge on the winning side.

Part of the game was to form alliances by marriage. Royal marriages were most important now that nations were growing so strong. A marriage was often better than a treaty—it might last longer. If powerful France could be encircled by Ferdinand's children on neighboring thrones, surely those thrones would be unfriendly to France for a long time. With this in mind, the Spanish princesses were married off to important foreign kings to the east, north, and west of France: the Portuguese, English, and Austrian kings.

Another great match was arranged for Crown Prince Juan, the only son of Ferdinand and Isabella, and the apple of their eye. They had the highest hopes for this match, but within a year Prince Juan was dead. Soon after, one daughter died and another became insane. A third daughter, married to king Henry VIII, lived on as queen of England.

Now a real blow came to Spain. Queen Isabella's health began to fail. The deaths of two children and the madness of another, the years of riding with the army over harsh country, the long days and late nights of attending to the affairs of state, now took their toll. Though she continued to rule conscientiously, she withdrew more and more to herself. Under her black dresses she wore a monk's scratchy robe. She wept and prayed for her lost children.

As she lay dying, she still gave audiences and dictated quantities of correspondence. Prayers for her recovery were said by her devoted subjects throughout the nation. Hundreds of pilgrimages were made to holy shrines, but to no avail. She died in 1504 at the age of fifty-three, in the thirtieth year of her reign. Spain had lost the person who was most responsible for its successful crusade against the Moors. Spain also owed the New World to her, for it was she who first offered to back Columbus and continued to give him encouragement and support.

Her enemies, the Moors, had justly feared her persistence and courage; the Jews had dreaded her ruthlessness. But her Christian subjects had truly loved her for her piety and her care for the poor.

Twelve years remained to Ferdinand—years of increasing conquest and discovery. Spanish ships were daily finding more land for him in the New World. A former fighter in the wars against the Moors, Ponce de Leon, now used his military talents in an expedition to Florida in 1513. Another Spanish soldier, Balboa, in that same year became the first European to see the Pacific Ocean. Central America, Peru, Colombia, Venezuela, the great Amazon and La Plata rivers—all were discovered by Spaniards in Ferdinand's lifetime. Treasure began to flow in from the New World, carried by great Spanish ships to the booming port of Seville.

Ferdinand even sent out an invasion fleet to the African coast, which captured the wealthy, fruitful towns of Oran, Algiers, and Tripoli. The conquerors liberated many Christian captives from the Moors and gathered more spoils and land for Spain.

Ferdinand died in 1516 at the age of sixty-four. His enterprises had been so vast that he had collected little treasure for himself; all his money had gone toward increased power and lands for Spain.

At his death Spain was the dominant state in Europe. The Spanish Empire included a third of Italy, the big islands of Sicily, Corsica, and Sardinia, parts of the northern coast of Africa, and a huge part of the New World. Thousands of impoverished Spanish peasants and hungry adventurers had left their scraggy soil to colonize these new lands and bring to them the Spanish religion and culture and habits. The Spanish army had been modernized into solid battalions with skilled leaders and powerful artillery—a far cry from the early days of Ferdinand's reign when individual knights charged their enemies with lance and sword.

Both King Ferdinand and Queen Isabella were remarkable rulers, governing with intelligence and constantly looking out for the good of their country. She was the more popular, he the more feared; she the more emotional, he the more crafty. As a ruling team they were unbeatable. True Renaissance rulers, they took advantage of the adventurous, expanding spirit of the times. At the start of their rule Spain was a little, divided, medieval land; at its end, she was the first great power of Renaissance Europe and the modern world.

The Spanish victory at Oran, in North Africa.

CHRISTOPHER COLUMBUS

Christopher Columbus.

In all of Ferdinand's and Isabella's reign, the most brilliant event was Christopher Columbus' discovery of America. Thanks to the persistence and courage of this great Italian navigator and the willingness of the Spanish sovereigns to take a gamble, a new world was opened up. Now Renaissance man could turn his enormous energies from the crowded lands of old Europe to new lands full of the promise of wealth and glory.

Columbus was born in Genoa, Italy, in 1451. He was about the same age as Lorenzo de' Medici, Leonardo da Vinci, and Ferdinand and Isabella. Like them, he took advantage of the spirit of the era, with its eagerness to absorb knowledge and to expand. Everyone in the middle of the fifteenth century was as interested in navigation and geography as we in the twentieth century are in electronics and space ships. Maps, ships, and instruments (though primitive in our eyes) had made a big step forward. Ancient geography manuscripts, rediscovered and translated by Renaissance scholars, became available to all. People read every geography book they could put their hands on. And every educated person in the fifteenth century knew that the world was a globe.

Columbus was lucky to be born in a century of such geographical curiosity and nautical progress. The times were ripening for daring explorations into unknown seas.

Genoa, where Columbus was born, was the ideal place to train the future Admiral of the Ocean Sea. At the time of his birth it was a thriving Italian city-state centered about a great port and busy harbor. As early as the thirteenth century Genoese galleys had taken crusaders and pilgrims across the Mediterranean to the Holy Land. There the Genoese captains met Arab captains who had sailed eastward across the Indian Ocean—using a compass, a magical device with a needle which always pointed north. These Arabs had returned with bales of silk and bags of spices; jewel chests of emeralds from India, rubies from Tibet and sapphires from Ceylon. The eyes of the Genoese popped with amazement. They started bartering with the Arabs for their rich cargoes of spices and gems. They also learned from the Arabs more about astronomy and navigation and mapmaking than had been known in all of Europe during the Middle Ages.

It was not long before Genoa became one of the great maritime powers of the Mediterranean, developing a series of trading colonies along the trade routes from Tunis in Africa to the northernmost shores of the Black Sea.

Down at the wharves of Genoa's beautiful blue harbor sheltered by high green hills, Columbus as a boy watched the shipwrights build sturdy merchant ships. Later he would see them sail out of the harbor, loaded with wool and linen cloth, metals and hides, their gaily painted sails puffed out like carnival balloons. Months later he would watch them return with spices, carpets, perfumes, and jewels from Genoese trading posts in the Near East.

Columbus longed to go on these ships. Though he helped his father in his small weaving business, his heart was not in this land-lubber trade. The lure of the sea was too much. Once in a while his father let him escape the chore of carding wool to go out with the little local fishing fleet for a night's catch of sardines, or to sail to the next village a few miles along the coast with a shipper of cheeses and wines.

After the day's work Columbus hung around the wharves and taverns to hear the sea captains' stories of their voyages. He never went to school, for it was not the custom for weavers' sons, but he got the best possible training for his future career from listening carefully to the captains and looking at their beautiful charts.

The sea captains liked this tall, redheaded boy with his flashing blue eyes and enthusiastic questions. They taught him all their lore. In the old days, they told him, it was a matter of guesswork to put out on the open Mediterranean Sea. There were no maps or compasses. It was much safer to hug the shore and keep it in sight as much as possible. Little books, instead of maps, guided the mariners of previous centuries. The books told the sailors to listen

Single-masted Mediterranean trader of the Middle Ages.

PIERPONT MORGAN LIBRARY

for somebody's cowbell on a certain coast or to look for three crooked trees on top of a certain cliff. But these directions were not much help if the cow died or the trees fell. The old mariners used to pray for the sun to stay out so that they could be sure of their direction during the day—or for the north star to shine clearly so that they could steer by it at night. And the old ships were so small and clumsily rigged, with single mast and square sail, that the captains had to go the way the wind was blowing or else let the sail down and call on their rowers. And so it had been for hundreds and hundreds of years.

But now, the Genoese captains said, what improvements! With more masts, more sails, and better rigging, a ship could sail closer to the wind and was far more navigable. With the new sheepskin sea charts showing coastlines, depths of anchorage, and distances from port to port, a sailor could navigate to a distant point with confidence. And there were instruments like the quadrant and the astrolabe which measured the angle made by three points: the sun (or Pole Star), the horizon, and the eye of the navigator; by looking up this angle in the latest astronomical tables, the navigator could find his latitude on an unknown sea or unknown shore. He was often inaccurate, because the sun was apt to blind him, the boat would rock, or the instrument might be faulty—but it was a great step forward nevertheless. Columbus learned to use the quadrant but never did master the rough astrolabe of the time.

As Columbus grew older he left his father's wool shop more and more to hire himself out as a hand on bigger ships. Twice he saw service in the Mediterranean against the Mohammedans—once against Moorish pirates from North Africa, another time defending the Genoese island of Chios against the fanatical Turks who were creeping westward across the Mediterranean and taking Genoa's possessions from her. Genoa's role as a great sea power was clearly doomed.

The Genoese shippers and merchants were worried about their future—they did not want Genoa to be a little, unimportant seaport full of memories but empty of trade. For two hundred years before the advent of the Turkish conquerors their ships had had peaceful trade with the caravans coming over desert and mountain to ports on the Mediterranean Sea. But now, they grumbled, the Turks met the caravans first, and then sold their cargoes to Christians only after adding outrageous taxes and profits. Some route to the Indies outside of Turkish control would have to be found, but it was clear that Genoa was neither powerful enough nor situated in the right place to search for such a route. Many Genoese decided to move to Portugal, which alone of all the European countries was trying to find a route to the Indies that would outflank the Mohammedans—a route by sea.

For fifty years Portuguese sailors had been venturing boldly southward along the African coast. By 1471 they had rounded its big northwestern bulge and discovered the rich Gold and Ivory Coasts (modern Guinea, Ghana, and Nigeria) reaching as far as the river Niger where Africa turns south again. In the same period of time they had found the nine islands of the Azores more than seven hundred miles out in the Atlantic. They colonized Madeira and the Cape Verde Islands, also many miles westward in the open ocean.

There was great opportunity in Portugal's capital city and seaport, Lisbon, for sailors and mapmakers and navigators. Among the many of Columbus' countrymen who decided to leave Genoa and make for Lisbon was Columbus' younger brother, Bartholomew, who determined to become rich there by making maps and charts.

One of the luckiest accidents of all time brought Columbus to Lisbon. In 1476 he sailed on a trading convoy of five ships from Genoa with a valuable cargo for Lisbon and points north. We can imagine his first glimpse of the Atlantic as the Genoese caravel went through the Straits of Hercules. Probably at that moment the Mediterranean shrank in his mind to an unchallenging puddle, and the Atlantic, huge and uncharted, stirred his imagination.

Whatever his musings might have been, they were violently interrupted when the entire Genoese fleet was attacked by an enemy fleet off the southern coast of Portugal. The ship on which Columbus was sailing sank, carrying many men with her. Columbus, though wounded by a bullet, managed to grab a piece of wreckage and swim six miles to the Portuguese coast. When his wound was partly healed (though the bullet was never removed) he made his way penniless to the beautiful, busy port of Lisbon, where his brother welcomed him and took him as partner in his chart-making shop.

Lisbon was the best place to learn all there was to know about Atlantic navigation. Columbus observed the cargoes that appeared on the Lisbon docks—pepper, slaves, elephant tusks, gold dust from the Guinea coast. The smell of the biscuit ovens baking supplies for long voyages, the sound of many languages, the sight of the beautiful sheepskin charts showing new rivers and shoals and landmarks on the African coast—all were intoxicating to him. Sailors from Barcelona, Antwerp, London, and Marseilles gathered in the taverns and swapped stories of cooking ostrich eggs in Guinea, seeing their first hippopotamus, or catching a shadowy sight of mysterious islands in the western Atlantic which somehow seemed to disappear as their ship approached them.

About two or three years after his arrival in Lisbon, Columbus fell in love. He first met his future bride when he was attending mass in a chapel near his chart shop. She was the daughter of a man who had helped the Portuguese colonize the Atlantic island of Madeira, about five hundred miles southwest of Lisbon. He was now dead, but his daughter, Doña Felipa, and her mother, the widowed Doña Isabel, showed Columbus the charts and notes he had made on his voyages. Columbus must have impressed the mother with his intelligence and good manners, for though she had high social connections and Columbus was a foreign nobody, she gave him permission to marry Doña Felipa.

The young couple spent their first year or so on the islands of Porto Santo and Madeira, thriving places of sugar mills and wineries. Here Columbus took careful note of the Atlantic winds and currents in this more southerly, warmer latitude. Once in a while storms coming from the west would bring in big, unfamiliar seed pods and odd exotic woods carved in strange ways. He thought these were proof that the lands and men of the Orient could not be very far to the west. But everyone else was too busy thinking about the daily progress eastward of the Portuguese to the Orient to pay much attention to Columbus' theories.

After the birth of their son, Diego, Columbus and his wife returned to Lisbon.

Now he went on longer voyages than he had ever been on before. One took him as far as Ireland and Iceland. In Ireland he saw two little boats drift in from the west with two odd-looking, flat-faced people in them; though we think now that they must have been Laplanders, he decided they were from Cathay, in the Orient. Again he was looking westward and feeling sure that the lands and people of the Orient lay close by. Another voyage took him to the African Gold Coast.

"Man of Asia." One of the oddities explorers expected to find.

FOLGER SHAKESPEARE LIBRARY, WASHINGTON

In between these Atlantic voyages, Columbus worked with his brother at their map-making shop. Here he would copy in careful detail the rough sketches brought in by sailors, and would drink in their information about winds, distances, and climates. Maps of all parts of the known world came under his eye. Some were accurate, others were not—particularly those made by monks in the Middle Ages when the works of the Greek astronomers and geographers were forgotten. The monks based their maps on what had been taught in the Bible; they decided that Jerusalem was at the center of the earth, and Paradise somewhere in the Ocean Sea. They drew sea-monsters, and men whose heads were in their chests, and ants in Africa as big as dogs. They said that near the equator there were no winds, that there were sea grasses that would entangle all ships, and that the Niger River boiled.

Columbus knew these maps were ridiculous. He had seen for himself that the Niger River did not boil and that the ants on its banks were not as big as dogs. He had not met any of the sea monsters drawn so realistically on the medieval maps, or got entangled in bottomless sea grasses, or been becalmed forever in the southern latitudes.

The best maps of the world that came his way were those of the ancient Greek geographers—men who had known from their astronomical observations that the earth was round, who had even guessed at its size, and who knew from the Arabs and the Egyptians about India and China. The maps and manuscripts of these men had been buried for more than a thousand years, hidden in medieval church libraries and monasteries—for they were considered too full of horrible pagan ideas to be read or studied. But now they had been rediscovered and translated into Latin by Renaissance scholars.

Columbus set himself to learn the Latin necessary to read these fascinating ancient geographies. One, written by the Greek Ptolemy more than thirteen hundred years before, intrigued him particularly. It was a best seller now; more than fifty editions rolled off the printing presses. In it were elaborate maps of twenty-six countries and a map of the world from the British Isles to the

Indian Ocean. It was full of inaccuracies, as Columbus knew from his own sailing experiences, but two things in the geography Columbus chose to believe: Ptolemy's estimate of the size of the globe (one sixth too small) and his estimate of the width of Asia (half again as wide as it really is). If the world were that small and Asia that wide, Columbus reasoned, there was not such a lot of ocean separating Asia from western Europe.

Then he read another best seller—Marco Polo's book of travels, now being printed at a great rate. Marco Polo had made his famous overland voyage from Venice to China early in the fourteenth century. Upon his return people had scoffed and laughed at his tales of the jeweled courts of the Great Khan of China and the golden roofs of Japan. But now, in Columbus' time, with the world opening up and something new being discovered every day, people were ready to believe that these old tales were not exaggerated. Marco's estimate of the width of Asia was two thousand miles greater than Ptolemy's estimate. He also added that Cipangu (Japan) lay fifteen hundred miles farther off the coast of China. When Columbus read this, the distance of the ocean from Portugal westward to Japan shrank even farther in his mind.

Columbus read more books to support his theory. He did some more figuring, shrinking the world a little more and stretching the land mass a little farther, and finally concluded that the Atlantic Ocean lying between Portugal and Japan would be about three thousand miles. And if he should make a first stop at one of the Portuguese islands in the Atlantic, like Madeira, that would cut off another five hundred. Twenty-five hundred miles was not such a terrifying distance, he thought, and with good ships and a good crew it ought not to take many days to get to Japan and the Indies.

He longed to put his conviction to the test, but ships and men were more than a mere map maker and navigator could afford. If he could convince one man—the King of Portugal—to underwrite this voyage, all would be well. The king was willingly spending a great deal of money to equip big expeditions exploring ever farther around Africa toward the Indies; surely he would have money to spare for a mission with a similar end in view—but by a much shorter route!

Armed with all the evidence and arguments he could collect, Columbus went to the King of Portugal in 1484 and asked for ships to take him the short distance westward to Japan.

The King of Portugal dashed Columbus' hopes, but not for the reasons legend would have us believe—that Columbus alone knew the world was round, while the old fogies who advised the king were sure it was flat. As we have seen, the geographers of Renaissance days knew very well that the world was round. And many of them had figured out, far more accurately than Columbus, just what the earth's circumference was, how wide Asia was, and how far away from Europe Japan should be.

Therefore when Columbus was turned down by the scientific advisers to the Portuguese king, it was *not* because they thought that the world was flat and Columbus and his ships would fall off the edge. Instead they thought that he could never make it to Japan, which they had figured (rightly) was about ten thousand miles to the west.

Spain was the next logical country for Columbus to approach. The Spanish coast faced the Atlantic for many long miles; her sailors too were experienced on the Atlantic, and had in fact colonized the Canary Islands some six hundred miles southwest of Spain. Columbus thought (and he was almost right) that the Canaries were in the same latitude as Japan, and would be a good place to sail to first on his way there—if he could get ships and permission from the Spanish monarchs.

In 1485, Columbus left Portugal, full of hope that King Ferdinand and Queen Isabella of Spain would listen with favor to his plan.

Taking his small son, Diego, with him, for his wife had died, he sailed around to the Spanish seaport of Palos. It was a small and ancient town, once Roman, whose white buildings stood on a cliff above the copper-colored river Tinto. His heart must have sunk as he compared this small port with thriving, cosmopolitan Lisbon. Because he had no money, he knocked hopefully at the door of a Franciscan monastery which stood six miles downriver on a high hill overlooking the broad estuary. Here he had his first night's rest in Spain.

The friars listened sympathetically as he told them his dream of the right way to go to the Indies. One can still see the stone cell in the monastery where Columbus spent the night. Guides still point to the well from which they say his ships' casks were filled seven years later at the start of their voyage to the New World, and even to some rusty rings where they say the *Niña, Pinta,* and *Santa Maria* were made fast.

The friars persuaded Columbus to leave his little boy with them while he went to Cordova in search of the Spanish sovereigns. As usual, they were on the move. The war with the Moors was in its fourth year, and the king and queen had to go from one place to another raising men and supplies. At the moment they were in Madrid. But on their return to Cordova in 1486 the fateful meeting between Columbus and the great Spanish monarchs took place.

The meeting went off well. All three of them were of the same age, in their mid-thirties, all vigorous, intelligent, and of strong personalities. Columbus' hard life with its many frustrations had paled his reddish hair, but he was a fine-looking man, tall, with a ruddy face, aristocratic nose, and piercing blue eyes. His coloring was, in fact, rather like the queen's—and so was his character. Both were very serious and religious; Columbus believed that he had been chosen by God to spread the faith in far heathen lands, as she believed that her war against the heathen Moors was God's will. He, like the queen, was modest in his dress and not interested in the gay times, great feasts, and hearty drinking of the court.

She was immediately sympathetic to him. His enthusiasm about his proposed trip appealed to her, for she too was an enthusiastic person. With her permission he outlined how easy the trip would be, what riches it would bring to Spain, and what hosts of pagans would be converted to Christianity.

King Ferdinand was not so attracted to him. The king was a very different man from this emotional, visionary foreigner. But Columbus obviously had some qualities in common with the king—

toughness, courage, and confidence. These must have secured the king's respect.

In spite of the good first impression that Columbus made, it was not a favorable time to put any proposition to the king and queen. They were enjoying their first successes in the project then dearest to their hearts—expelling the Moors. They had the backing of the entire nation and enough money, for once, to prosecute the war. If Columbus had come forward with an idea for a new cannon or an explosive land mine, they might have given him generous sums to get on with it. As it was, their minds were preoccupied. Ships? Provisions? Men? The king and queen needed all their ships to harry the Moorish ports and bring in supplies from other countries. They were simply not interested in sparing any provisions or extra men for a totally new project. But they did not turn Columbus down flat, as had the King of Portugal. They gave him a small salary and they appointed a group of scholars to look into his proposal.

This delay, so inconsequential to them, was a frightful prospect for the impatient Columbus. Every time a big Moorish city fell to the Spanish, Columbus' hopes would rise—now the king and queen would give him their attention. But on the contrary the sovereigns would be all the more eager for another victory over the Moors. Columbus was also having a difficult time at court where his ridiculous, impractical proposition was laughed at. The raised eyebrows, the yawns, the snubs of courtiers became unbearable to the proud Columbus. In 1488 he decided to turn again to Portugal, encouraged by a surprisingly hearty invitation from the Portuguese king. The latter more than a year before had sent his greatest captain, Bartholomew Dias, to find the tip of Africa, but nothing had been heard from him. Perhaps, thought the Portuguese king, Africa had no end; perhaps, as some of the ancient maps said, it was a solid land mass enclosing the Indian Ocean. If this were the case, the Portuguese were wasting their time. Maybe that Genoese foreigner's idea of a short trip westward to the Indies would be more practical after all.

Columbus' hopes soared as he headed back to Portugal. But

his timing was bad again. In the same month, December 1488, that he reached Lisbon, Bartholomew Dias sailed back into Lisbon Harbor with the breath-taking news that he had rounded the wide, southernmost end of Africa—and that the way eastward across the Indian Ocean to the wealth of the Indies lay open to the Portuguese nation. Now, of course, the Portuguese king saw no need to risk ships on an unknown western course.

Back to Spain with a heavy heart went Columbus. He had another four years to wait there. During this time he read again and again all the geography books, old and new, that would reinforce his theories. All the books talked of the seas of pearls, the precious stones, and the golden-tiled roofs of the oriental monarchs. Even the Bible, with its tales of King Solomon's riches from the Orient—ivory, apes, and peacocks, and gold and precious stones from Ophir—whetted his appetite and strengthened his purpose. At the same time he fretted to think that the Bible's sacred places were now in the hands of the Turk. He longed to reach the Indies, convert the natives, and thus surround the wicked Mohammedans with vast Christian empires.

In 1490, Ferdinand's and Isabella's advisers, after deliberating for five years, announced that Columbus' project was "vain and worthy of rejection." They reasoned, as the Portuguese scientists had reasoned, that the distance across the Atlantic was far longer than Columbus so confidently stated. Besides, they added, three fifths of the world was uninhabitable and most of the ocean unnavigable. What was more, God could not possibly have created lands yet unknown to man—so the prospect of any islands to help him en route was silly. Even Isabella, Columbus' great protector, was impressed by their argument.

Completely discouraged, Columbus now decided to try his fortunes in France. He set off, but first stopped to pick up his son at the monastery in Palos. Fray Juan Perez, the head of the monastery, was shocked at the way his old friend had been treated, and resolved to do something about it. He had never forgotten those enthusiastic talks in the early days when Columbus had first arrived, and he had waited impatiently for the day when his friend would sail down the river below the monastery walls, to prove his theories on the beckoning Atlantic.

Brother John had once been confessor to the queen. He knew her heart, and the words to move it. No one knows to this day what those words were, but after her meeting with the persuasive friar she was convinced again. She summoned Columbus, sending him money to buy a mule and proper clothing, for Brother John had painted a sad picture of his poverty.

In 1491, Columbus on his new mule arrived at Santa Fe, the remarkable city the sovereigns had built so quickly before the walls of Moorish Granada. Here the king and queen were directing the steps of the final siege of the war. A few months later, in January of 1492, Columbus was on his knees among the spellbound watchers as the dejected Moorish king rode out of the gates for the last time and the huge silver cross and the banners of Spain replaced the Moorish crescent on the red battlements. Now surely the triumphant king and queen could give him their undivided attention—and, more important, money and ships and men.

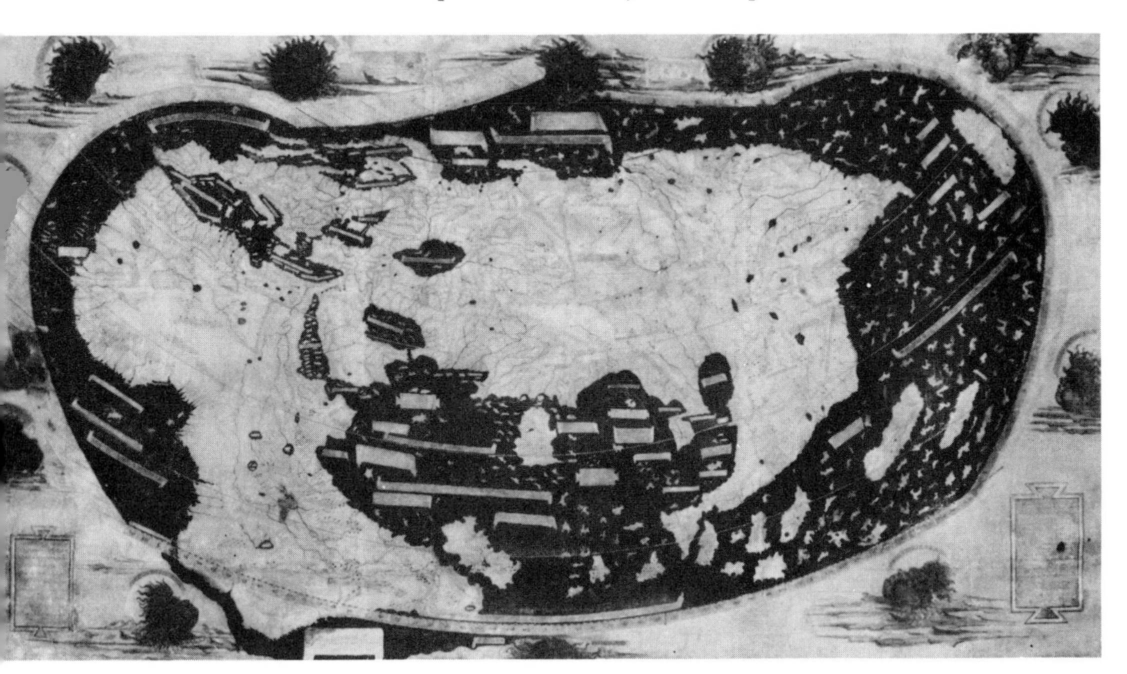

A rare map, drawn about 1489, soon after Diaz rounded the tip of Africa. Columbus possibly studied it. Note the wide land area and the narrow ocean, with no America between Spain and China.

YALE UNIVERSITY LIBRARY

Columbus decided that, since he had been treated badly in the past when he had demanded little, he might as well demand a great deal this time: titles, a coat of arms for himself and his descendants forever, and a large percentage of the riches he might discover. For a while these demands outraged King Ferdinand and Queen Isabella—particularly the thrifty king—and almost ruined Columbus' last chances in Spain. But fortunately a powerful court official intervened for him. Luis de Santangel, one of King Ferdinand's treasurers, went to the queen. It was quite unlike her, he said, after she had been so unwavering for ten years about the expensive and risky venture of the Moorish war, to be timid now about a relatively inexpensive project like this one. What was there to lose? A few small ships, a little money, few men—nothing to compare with her risks and expenses to date. What was there to gain? Everything! New lands and riches and subjects for Spain, new Christian converts for the glory of God. The Portuguese were on their way to the Indies; any day, now, they would get to fabled Calicut. This would be a chance for Spain to get there ahead of them. And on no account should Columbus make such a voyage for the hated King of France and perhaps bring *him* the wealth of the Indies!

We can imagine that King Ferdinand's ears pricked up when the queen relayed this particular argument to him. But it was the queen who was especially persuaded. Never as practical as her husband, more emotional and warm, she had always been touched by Columbus' passionate sincerity. She offered to pledge her jewels if necessary to send him on his way.

Once the sovereigns made their decision, things moved fast. Documents were drawn up, making Columbus Admiral of the Ocean Sea and viceroy over all islands and mainlands that he might discover. They assigned him a tenth of the gold and jewels and spices he would find. Upon a successful crossing, he would be permitted to call himself "Don" Cristobal Colon—the title of a gentleman.

They also gave him a sort of passport to identify himself to the Grand Khan or any other prince he might find in the Indies.

Model of the Santa Maria.

ADDISON GALLERY OF AMERICAN ART,
PHILLIPS ACADEMY, ANDOVER

Then they sent him to the port of Palos, with orders to the townspeople to outfit him with three ships, crews, and supplies. Columbus arrived in Palos in May 1492. In ten weeks, in August, he was ready to go.

The ships chartered for the voyage were the *Niña,* the *Pinta,* and the *Santa Maria*—the admiral's flagship. No one knows exactly what they looked like, or how long, wide, or deep they were. We know that the *Niña* was of about sixty tons—which in those days meant that she could carry sixty barrels (tuns) of wine below decks. The *Pinta* was about the same size. The *Santa Maria* was the largest—maybe one hundred tons. Certainly they were not the frail cockleshells of legend, but well built by experienced shipbuilders who had sailed on voyages to Africa and England and knew how to build the kind of ship that could tackle the Atlantic Ocean. Each ship had three masts—the mainmast as long as the ship, the other two masts only a third as long. All had huge square mainsails, smaller foresails, and triangular mizzens after the Arab fashion. Two of the ships had a small sail hung on the bowsprit, and the

Santa Maria had a topsail over the lookout's perch. All the sails were decorated with special green crosses designed by Columbus, with the crowns and initials of Ferdinand and Isabella painted above the arms of the crosses.

Each ship carried one heavy lifeboat and a few pieces of artillery—the awkward lombards that would throw stone cannon balls, and some smaller guns. Except for a few clumsy muskets, these were all the arms Columbus had to conquer Japan or any other heathen country foolish enough to resist the demands of a Christian admiral from Spain.

There were a few important instruments on board—the compass, quadrant, astrolabe, and mathematical tables that recorded the positions of sun and stars at certain times of night and day all the days of the year. There was also the half-hour glass which the ship's boy had to be sure to turn the instant the sands ran out.

Ninety men were enlisted for the fleet, most of them local men and boys, good sailors—not the jailbirds and ruffians of legend. They were the best that Palos and the neighboring towns could provide, and they had courage, experience, and skill. The king and queen sent two royal officers along to keep an eye on things; there was also an interpreter, who, because he spoke Arabic and Hebrew, was supposed to be able to converse easily with the Grand Khan of China. A silversmith was attached to the crew to supervise the washing of the gold that was sure to be found in every hill and stream of the Indies.

The day of departure came—August 3, 1492—for the greatest voyage of all time, a voyage that was to change the history of the world. Many have said that on this day the Middle Ages ended and the modern world began.

Columbus spent much of the previous night in prayer. Before dawn he went on board the flagship and gave the orders to cast off. Wives huddled sorrowfully together on the banks in the darkness; children raced along the edge of the river as the three ships floated downstream with the ebb tide. The barefooted sailors waved their caps and called good-by as long as they could. When the voyagers passed the monastery of La Rabida and heard the monks singing the early morning prayer they crossed themselves and prayed for God's help on the unknown seas ahead.

Soon the sea breeze caught them at the harbor's edge and their sails filled. During the whole day the three little ships could be seen from the land, making their way offshore before setting course southwest for the Canary Islands, the last known stop before Japan.

On August 12 they anchored at the Canaries. There they made repairs and changed some rigging. They filled the water casks, brought in more firewood, and stored fresh vegetables and meat, and cheese for fast days. By September 8 they were off again, but not until the ninth did they see the last of familiar land behind them—the highest mountain peak of the islands, sinking gradually below the horizon. Sometime that afternoon they saw nothing on any side of them but the great ocean. From now on no one's charts or advice or experience could guide them. All they had to go on was the admiral's courage, faith in God, and unswerving belief in an untried theory.

Then welcome northeasterly winds filled their sails and continued to blow the little fleet those twenty-four hundred miles that Columbus estimated lay between the Canary Islands and Japan. Thirty-three days later, on October 12, 1492, the fleet had

The first landing of Columbus.

covered just about that number of miles. Before Columbus' grateful eyes stretched the green tropical Bahama Island of San Salvador—just in time, for the crew lacked their admiral's confidence and were threatening to turn back. Columbus of course was convinced that he had landed on the outskirts of Japan—part of "the Indies"—in that short sail, and that the natives who greeted him were "Indians."

For five months he sailed among the islands of the Caribbean Sea. He took Cuba to be the mainland of Cathay. Here for the first time Europeans saw men smoking tobacco and sleeping in woven beds called hamacas. They also saw enough gold ornaments on the natives to assume that there were gold mines over the next hill—or the next. When the flagship *Santa Maria* was wrecked on a coral reef just before the return voyage, thirty-nine of the men gladly stayed behind to look for these gold mines. The rest sailed back in the two smaller ships, Columbus in his second flagship, the *Niña*.

At sunrise of March 15, 1493, fishermen in the estuary of Palos and workers in the fields saw a small dot on the horizon; as it drew nearer they could hardly believe their eyes. It was the *Niña,* battered by storms, paint worn off her hull, her sails patched and faded, but still making brave headway. Crowds gathered by the river edge, and neighbors hurried over the marshes from the neighboring villages. By midday Columbus had come in with the flood tide over the sand bar at the river's mouth. By afternoon he was made fast. With shrieks of joy the families were reunited with the bearded sailors. The monks of La Rabida hastened along the shore of the river to welcome Columbus and offer him hospitality once more. But what a change! Instead of a penniless chart maker, their guest now was the triumphant Don Cristobal Colon, Admiral of the Ocean Sea, viceroy and governor of the islands of the Indies.

News flashed eight hundred miles across the country to the sovereigns at Barcelona, who sent him an enthusiastic letter, desiring him to come to them as fast as possible. All along his way to their court swarmed the people to see him pass by—city dwellers on the rooftops, farmers leaving their green spring fields to stare at the elegantly dressed admiral and his exotic cargo: six odd-looking, bronze-skinned men decorated in feathers and paint; chattering monkeys, gaudy parrots, ornaments of that much-sought-after metal, gold.

In triumph Columbus arrived at the court of the king and queen. The nobles who had mocked him now rushed to greet him; Ferdinand and Isabella rose to offer him a place of honor by their side.

A letter that Columbus had sent to the sovereigns on his return was immediately printed in Barcelona. It gave vivid descriptions of the New World. "In it are very many ranges of hills," he wrote, "and most lofty mountains . . . all most beautiful in a thousand shapes, and all accessible, and full of trees of a thousand kinds, so lofty that they seem to reach the sky. And I am assured that they never lose their foliage; as may be imagined, since I saw them as green and beautiful as they are in Spain during May. And some of them were in flower, some in fruit . . . and the nightingale was singing, and other birds of a thousand sorts, in the month of November . . . Española is a marvel: the mountains and hills, and plains and fields, and the soil, so beautiful and rich for planting and sowing, for breeding cattle of all sorts, for building of towns and villages. There could be no believing, without seeing, such harbors as are here, as well as the many and great rivers, and excellent waters, most of which contain gold." It was a land, Columbus added urgently, "to be desired, and once seen, never to be relinquished."

This letter was printed and reprinted in all the big cities of Europe. It became the best seller of the day.

Men were wildly excited by the new discoveries. Their curiosity and imagination and dreams of glory, so characteristic of Renaissance days, grew to a high pitch. Now they could plant colonies and build new cities, find gold mines and convert savages.

The fifteenth century had been full of exciting events, and Columbus' discovery was its crowning one.

France
in the time of
Francis I & Rabelais
0 50 100 150 Miles
SCALE
ENGLAND
Dover
Calais
English Channel
Rhine R.
Seine R.
Reims
Paris
Metz
Brittany
Fontainebleau
Orléans
Atlantic
Ocean
Loire River
Chambord
Amboise
Chinon
Fontenay le Comte
Poitiers
Vienne River
Charente R.
Cognac
Angoulême
N
FRANCE
Burgundy
Saône R.
Lyons
Switzerland
Alps Mountains
Battles of
Marignano
& Pavia
Milan
Turin
Po River
Rhône R.
Montpellier
Marseilles
Pyrenees Mountains
SPAIN
Mediterranean
Sea
ITALY

PART 3
FRANCE AWAKES

A French castle on a hill and fertile valley below.

FRENCH GOVERNMENT TOURIST OFFICE

WHEN the Renaissance was at its peak in Italy, France was recovering from a long-drawn-out war with England. Like Spain, she was changing from a feudal country of many little principalities into a united nation.

France lies to the north of Spain. Her natural boundaries enclose a beautiful and fertile land, blessed by a temperate climate which is never too hot or too cold.

Though smaller than Texas, the land of France is much more varied. The snow-capped Alps on its eastern border boast the highest alpine peak, Mont Blanc. To the south lie the warm Mediterranean and the rugged Pyrenees Mountains. To the west stretches the Atlantic Ocean, washing the shores of France on beautiful beaches and rocky ledges much like the Maine coast line. To the north the English Channel and the North Sea, and to the northeast the Rhine River, complete the natural boundaries which almost encircle this country.

Many beautiful rivers irrigate France's fertile land. Generations of men cleared forests, drained swamps, and cultivated the fields. The wonderful productive soil of France which grows wheat, corn, grapes, and olives in such abundance was the result of man's labor.

France has been called *la belle france.* A medieval historian once said, "Next to the Kingdom of Heaven, France is the fairest kingdom on earth." It is still a most beautiful country whose cities are adorned with lovely Gothic cathedrals, whose countryside is dotted with graceful châteaux.

With its exposure on so many seas and navigable rivers, France was an easy prey to invaders. The Romans invaded it from the Mediterranean and finally, under the leadership of Julius Caesar, conquered it. A great Roman civilization flourished there until barbarians from the north plunged it into the darkness that descended on Europe. Continued barbarian invasions and later wars with England kept France divided through the Dark and Middle Ages. The kings' struggles to unify France were also delayed by the warring feudal nobles.

The devastating war between France and England from the middle of the fourteenth century to the middle of the fifteenth century was known as the Hundred Years' War. It took the inspiration of a medieval peasant girl, Joan of Arc, to lead France toward victory and unity. In 1453, when the English were finally driven from the shores, the fair land of France lay barren and exhausted. The fertile farms, ruined by the English, had gone back to forests. The saying was, "The forests came back to France through the English." All was wasteland; wolves prowled in the outskirts of Paris, bands of lawless knights plundered and killed with unchecked violence.

But France has always had amazing powers of recovery and she now settled down to building and shaping a nation. Louis XI, who came to the throne in 1461, was responsible for making a nation out of France. Known as the Spider, he was devious and cruel, but he knew what was good for his country. He ruled by intrigue and fear. Craftily he spread his net, catching now one, then another rebellious noble until he caught them all.

Charles VIII entering Naples in 1494.

ALINARI PHOTO

By 1477, France was a united kingdom and the nobles, no longer important in their strongholds, flocked to the court to gain the favor of the king. Prosperity returned to the country as farms were made fertile once more. Towns flourished under King Louis' encouragement of industry, his introduction of silk weaving and the first printing presses in France.

Louis XI and his two successors, Charles VIII and Louis XII, paved the way for the French Renaissance. Charles, nourished on chivalric romances in his youth, had the grandiose ideas of a conquering hero. Casting his eyes on the wealthy peninsula, Italy, he set out in 1494 to capture Naples. Duke Lodovico of Milan, at war with Naples, even urged him to come. With this opening of the gates to the foreigner began the downfall of Italy. Henceforth she would be a battleground for greedy foreign nations.

The French easily captured Naples but no sooner were they installed there than all Italy, with the help of Spain, turned against them and chased them back to France. This adventure gained nothing for France in a material way but it did something far more important. It brought her into contact with the Italian Renaissance.

Inspired by the beauty and elegance of Italian buildings and gardens, Charles began to change the old royal castle at Amboise from a fortified stronghold into a lovely palace. He enlarged the windows to let in light and built beautiful gardens, adorned with fountains. He inspired others to build châteaux on the Loire River not far from Paris.

Louis XII, who succeeded Charles, was known as the father of his people for his many reforms, his reduction of taxes and repression of bandits. Yet in spite of his wisdom he too could not resist that prize of wealth and art, Italy.

Again with an impressive army the French went over the Alps, this time to capture Milan as well as to retake Naples. King Louis met Leonardo da Vinci in Milan. He was so impressed by the artist's *Last Supper* that he wanted to remove it, wall and all, and take it back to France.

Pope Julius II, who had once said, "Don't put a book in my hand, give me a sword," was ready to go to war to drive out these foreigners. To do this he made an alliance with Ferdinand of Spain and Henry VIII of England, and in 1513 the French were again forced out of Italy. In the last battle of this little war the French nobles fled so fast that it was called "The Battle of the Spurs."

These victories and defeats in Italy did not gain France any new territories. But for a second time the breath of the Italian Renaissance was blown northward. While France was plundering Italy, Italy was educating her in new ideas, in art and literature, and in how to live. However, the Italian Renaissance would not have affected France had she not been ready for a Renaissance of her own.

France was now a unified nation, rich and prosperous. Her energies, so wasted in the long war with England, were now ready to burst forth in other directions. She was starting on her road to fame, to be a leader among nations in the cultivation of art, literature, and beauty, above all in the art of living. She was ready to absorb all the new influences and ideas which came her way.

With the next king, Francis I, the French Renaissance reached its peak.

FRANCIS I

Francis I by Titian.

ALINARI PHOTO

IN 1515, Francis, a true Renaissance prince, came to the French throne. Not so crafty as Ferdinand, not so clever as Lorenzo, Francis nevertheless aspired to fame and power. But he wanted so many other things from life—joy, beauty, and adventure—that he could not concentrate on power alone. He gave a new luster and meaning to the kingly office, which was just what France wanted. Tired of her old infirm kings, France welcomed this handsome, gay young prince who wanted to drink in all that life could offer. He was the very spirit of the new Renaissance in France.

Francis I, cousin of Louis XII, was born in 1494 in the lovely little town of Cognac, nestled in the vine-growing valley of the Charente River. Near the river the old moated castle, long the home of the dukes of Angoulême, was still an imposing fortress from without. Yet it was changing. Larger windows were replacing the medieval slits, staircases and balconies were beginning to adorn the courtyard. Here, in an atmosphere not of luxury but of gracious living, Francis was surrounded by his mother, sister, and female relatives. They all adored him and he adored himself. Showered with affection and adulation, he was spoiled beyond measure. He learned early to command but could not bear criticism. But he was by nature gay and lively, generous and brave, and so made friends easily. Besides love and indulgence, Francis was surrounded by art, books, and music. He seemed to be born with a sense of beauty and loved beauty passionately all his life—beautiful art and music and beautiful women.

His mother, Louise, was not only a doting mother; she was also a clever and ambitious woman. As a child she had had a taste of court life and she longed for the glamor and luxury of such a life. She knew that if King Louis and his queen had no heir, her son, as next of kin, might one day be king. A fortuneteller had increased her hopes by prophesying that she would bear a son who would be king. Dreaming of future riches and power, Louise observed with glee the sad death after death of Louis XII's infant sons. When the queen died, Louise felt triumphant. Surely her little Caesar, as she called Francis, would be king, if only nothing happened to him in the meantime. She scarcely ever left his side for fear something would. If only the old king would die! But Louis' old infirm body held onto life a long time. He even married again, young Mary Tudor, sister of Henry VIII of England. Louise was frantic. There still might be a direct heir to the throne.

When Francis was about five years old his family moved to the royal castle of Chinon, a medieval fortress high above the Vienne River, and Francis began his education as a young nobleman of royal blood. He learned the arts of jousting, hunting, and falconry. Old King Louis held court here at times and Francis often saw visiting noblemen and ambassadors from other countries. One day, standing on the ramparts of the lofty fortress, he watched with excitement the approach of an Italian prince, Cesare Borgia, and his sumptuous cavalcade. This dashing Italian courtier was coming to visit King Louis. Francis had never seen such an impressive sight. First came the pack mules covered with red and yellow satins and laden with chests, then the war horses, glittering with jeweled trappings. Silver trumpets and clarions sounded as Cesare Borgia, astride a huge charger draped in red satin edged with pearls, rode over the bridge and up the winding road to the castle. As Francis looked down on this prince he thought he had never seen anyone so fine, so handsome and with such soldierlike bearing. Cesare, lavishly dressed in the latest Italian fashion of brocaded satins edged with jewels, seemed to Francis the perfect cavalier. Francis was impressed. Where was this Italy and who were these wealthy Italians? King Louis must have seemed plain and old in contrast to this gay young cavalier, the castle of Chinon a gloomy place to entertain him in.

But Francis did not stay in Chinon long. The king had him moved to Amboise, the castle recently transformed by Charles VIII into a lovely château. Here Francis continued his education in skill at arms. Here also was a fine library, beautiful gardens, and a tennis court. Young nobles of Francis' age gathered here and joined him in games of athletic skill and the exciting hunt for stags and boars.

Though medieval chivalry was dead, its romance lingered on and Francis was more interested in the stories of King Arthur and his knights than he was in learning Latin or mathematics. He dreamed of glorious deeds of bravery in which he, a gallant knight, would be the center of attraction.

At the age of twelve Francis was betrothed to King Louis' daughter Claude. He now began to live like a real prince. He was given a retinue of waiting men: men-at-arms, a personal drummer, a falconer, and a secretary. His mother and his sister were equally honored with ladies in waiting and innumerable servants.

Francis developed into a tall, handsome youth, square-shouldered and athletically built. His hair was black, his nose large and long. His mischievous eyes and upturned eyebrows gave him the look of a gay devil.

He began to dress lavishly in satins and furs. He had not forgotten that richly dressed Italian prince, Cesare Borgia. His fine hands were always bedecked with rings. He usually wore a velvet beret with a plume held in place by a large diamond or ruby. Beneath his outer splendor he wore embroidered underwear which puffed out through slits in his satin blouses, showing its lacy elegance. He was heavily perfumed. His spurs were of gold and his sword was encased in a jeweled scabbard.

Francis liked to show off not only in flashy costumes but also in deeds of courage and skill. During some festivities at Amboise, Francis got his chance. To thrill the audience a wild boar was let loose in the courtyard. He was supposed to attack dummies, dangling on ropes in lifelike fashion. But the poor beast, bewildered and frantic, trying to escape, dashed up the stairs to the gallery where Francis was watching. Pushing through the guards who tried to stay him and the women shrieking with fear, Francis rushed toward the stairway. Aglow with excitement and the thrill of adventure, he brandished his sword to meet the oncoming boar. With true aim he thrust his sword into the beast's gaping jaws. The boar reared up, staggered, and plunged to the foot of the stairs with a resounding thud. The spectators gasped in fear and admiration for their brave young prince.

Above all other pastimes Francis loved the hunt. "No matter how old and ill I may be," he later said, "I will have myself carried to the hunt. And when I die I shall want to go there in my coffin." Throughout Europe hunting was the sport of kings, nobles, and even Popes. Huge forests were preserved just for the kings' pleasure. Hunting for stags or wild boars was the most exciting of all and Francis loved it for its dangerous thrills and skill of horsemanship. Astride his noble bay, Francis would sound the signal for departure. It was a stately procession at first. Francis, surrounded by his favorite nobles, was followed by archers and masters of the

Hunting for stags.

THE METROPOLITAN MUSEUM OF ART, WHITTELSEY FUND, 1949

hounds, leading the excited dogs on leashes. Noblewomen, some carried in litters, some on foot, and a few bold ones on horseback, followed in the rear. The excitement increased as they neared the forest and the dogs got the scent. Unleashed, they dashed ahead, baying loudly. The archers began to run. Francis and his nobles spurred their horses. The hunt had begun and as the men disappeared into the forest the ladies turned back toward the palace to await their return. They could hear the notes of the hunters' bugles, echoing through the woodland.

Plunging through underbrush, racing under trees or out across open fields and streams, the hunters pursued their game until the yelping dogs held it at bay.

It was during a hunt that Francis became separated from his companions. Resting by a tree, he gazed at the ground and noticed a small wounded creature, a little salamander. Its leg had been cut off but a new one was beginning to grow. Francis mused on this lizard and its power to revive and renew itself. Impressed, he made the salamander the emblem on his royal coat of arms, the symbol of victory after defeat.

In 1515 the old King Louis lay dying. He knew that his gay, extravagant young cousin would succeed him. "All our work is useless, this great boy will ruin everything," he sighed and then closed his eyes.

At the age of twenty-one Francis was anointed king in the beautiful Gothic cathedral of Rheims. Here all French kings had been anointed since 496 when Clovis, first king of the Franks, had been given the title of the Most Christian King of France. The coronation procession was gay as it wound its way into the town of Rheims. First came the archers, then the burghers in black and crimson velvet, then members of the trade guilds in bright colors, the generals, chamberlains, officers of the law, and the King's Council. His bodyguard carried the royal banners decorated with the golden salamander. The king's seal in a casket of blue and gold was borne on high by page boys. Nobles of the robe carried the royal cap covered with fleurs-de-lys, the cloak, and the jeweled sword. Then came Francis astride a white horse with silver harness inlaid with precious stones.

Salamander, emblem of Francis I, symbol of victory after defeat.

Before the altar in the dimly lit cathedral where colored light filtered through the stained-glass windows, Francis was made King of France. His mother and sister gazed with rapture at this handsome king. All their dreams had come true and all France rejoiced with them.

The festivities following his anointment went on for days. Masquerades, ballets, banquets, and sham battles entertained the court.

Now that Francis was king he could satisfy his extravagant and luxurious tastes. Soon after his coronation Francis took the first of his many migrations, which involved moving the entire court from one pleasure palace to another. With him went officers of the crown, courtiers, ladies of the court, ambassadors, archers, huntsmen, hounds, artists, musicians, poets, priests, doctors, cooks, and even furnishings. It was like moving an entire village; it took three thousand horses and mules to transport this vast entourage. Sometimes Francis and his favorite courtiers and ladies, accompanied by musicians, went by barge down the Loire River.

Under Francis court life developed a magnificence and splendor which surpassed even Florence and Milan. A distinctive feature of Francis' court was the prestige he gave to women. "A court without women is like a garden without flowers," he once remarked and his court sparkled with gay, beautiful ladies.

Francis loved music and had two groups of musicians. The court musicians often accompanied poets, ballets, and dances. They used harps, violas, lutes, spinets, and small portable organs. The second group played marching songs for royal processions; fifes, drums, tambourines, trumpets, and oboes made up this military band.

The expense of this court life with its constant journeyings from one pleasure spot to another was tremendous. Francis did not worry. He was king and would act like a king. The people did not worry either. In fact they enjoyed the splendor of the court. Whenever it came to a town everyone turned out to see the great procession. For the common people whose lives had little glamor, this court on the move was a gay pageant, a source of entertainment.

It was not surprising that Francis, eager for adventure as well as gaiety, turned his eyes toward Italy as his predecessors had done. Sure of success, he thought of the fun and excitement of an Italian war. He had heard of the wonderful buildings and art in Milan. He would like, and he determined to have, Milan. It would call for money, even more money than his luxurious court life; but he would leave that problem to his chancellor. There was no problem with his young nobles. Schooled like Francis in the art of jousting and tilting, they were as eager as he for an adventure in Italy.

There was one quick easy way to get money. Louis XII and many Renaissance Popes had practiced it. That was to sell offices, political positions, and titles of nobility. Rich merchants and lawyers, eager to become dukes and counts, spent large sums for this easy rise to political and social prestige. Nobles of ancient aristocracy resented this short cut to nobility but their protests went unheeded. New nobles flooded the royal court and new officers swelled the high court of justice. The treasury began to fill up.

In 1515, the very year he came to the throne, Francis made elaborate plans to retake Milan, which Louis XII had lost in 1513. He had the largest army and the best artillery in Europe and he wanted to show the Western world that he was its most important king. He managed to secure a promise of help from Venice, ever eager to suppress its rival, Milan.

Francis' schemes were soon learned by Italian, Spanish, and English spies. Henry VIII of England was watching this new young king jealously. Crafty old Ferdinand knew just what was going on. Even Pope Leo in Rome had wind of it.

Francis went to the flourishing town of Lyons, center of trade and banking, the gathering place for his army. His nobles of the sword made up the cavalry. The infantry, armed with pike, crossbow, and the new clumsy arquebus (an early form of gun), numbered twenty-six thousand French and German mercenaries. There were three hundred pieces of artillery; some of these were small bronze cannon which could shoot fifty bullets at once. Three thousand workers were hired to build roads, bridges, and trenches.

Each noble had his own company of soldiers. The constable, like a modern commander-in-chief, was the head of the French army.

Francis had bestowed this honor on his cousin Charles, Duke of Bourbon, a powerful noble who vied with Francis in wealth and popularity. Charles of Bourbon had a brooding though handsome face. Owner of vast lands and great wealth, he was a leftover from the days of feudalism. He wanted to assert his power and he resented this new, absolute monarch. He was a dark cloud on the horizon of this joyous reign.

But in July 1515, Francis was not worried about anything. His splendid army in blazing armor, gaily plumed, with banners flying, was ready to set off across the Alps with the utmost confidence. Francis surveyed his army with a smile of approval. The dummers started to drum, the fifers to blow. The colorful army started to move. All foretold success.

To get to Milan meant moving the vast French army over the Alps. Knowing that the enemy was alerted and waiting on the other side of the usual passes, the French undertook a daring plan. They decided to cross the mountains on an impracticable, dangerous route, known only to hunters. There were no towns nearby to provision the troops. The pass was full of such hazards as ravines and sudden avalanches. In places it became a mere ledge overhanging a deep abyss. To attempt to get an army of this size with horses and cannon over the wild alpine pass seemed madness. But to Francis and his young nobles it was a challenging adventure. In some spots the guns and cannon had to be slung by ropes, piece by piece, from one footing to another. Climbing and stumbling, the troops slowly made their way. One false step was followed by a cry and crashing of stones as horse and man plunged down a chasm. It took the army five days to get over those jagged, lonely peaks. But this bold effort proved worth while. The French arrived unnoticed by the enemy and were able to rush on toward the Po River and take one Italian army by surprise. Constable Bourbon commanded the advance guard, Francis the center or main army, and his brother-in-law the rear. They raced on toward Milan and camped at Marignano on a dusty plain a few miles north of the city.

Inside Milan, the Italian army, made up mostly of Swiss pike-

King Francis at Battle of Marignano.

GIRAUDON

men hired by the Milanese, fretted and worried. Should they surrender or rush out to meet this formidable French army? In Rome, Pope Leo fretted more. One army had already been taken without a struggle. It looked bad for Italy. Somehow the French king must be stopped. Leo dispatched messages to Spain and England.

Late in the afternoon of September 13, as Francis was trying on his new German armor, a noble rushed into his tent, shouting, "Sire, spread the alarm, the enemy advances."

Quickly the king put on his plumed helmet, picked up his lance, and mounted his war horse. Swiftly he galloped to the vanguard to see that all was ready. The enemy, whose best soldiers were Swiss mercenaries, could now be seen. The Swiss were rugged men of the mountains and they knew no fear. Shouting and yelling, they charged, with their pikes thrust forward, right into the French vanguard. Stunned by the force of their blows, the French fell back.

From atop his horse Francis could see glimpses of shining armor through the swirling dust. It was hard to tell what was happening and the sun was beginning to sink. Francis, leading his cavalry and shouting "France," rushed into the midst of the battle, thrusting right and left with his lance. The Swiss recoiled at this onslaught but soon, with reinforcements, they pushed the French back toward their artillery. Now the only light was a pale moon which shone down on the confused battlefield where charge and countercharge accounted for many dead. At eleven the moon went under the clouds and a truce was declared for the moment. The exhausted fighters tried to find their comrades in the cold damp mist which had spread over the marshes.

Francis was stunned, battered by blows of pike and lance. This war that he had longed for was a bloodier adventure than he had expected. His throat was parched and he asked for a drink of water. But when he swallowed the canal water which his drummer brought him he vomited. The water was mixed with blood. Still in armor, he threw himself on a gun carriage and slept fitfully until dawn.

The fighting had already begun when Francis awoke. The fierce courageous Swiss were attacking from all sides. The rear of the French army was giving away, exposing the king and his cavalry, when the thunderous approach of galloping horses was heard. The Venetians had arrived just in time to reinforce the French. Charging the Swiss, they forced them into the woods. The artillery boomed, the woods caught fire, and many Swiss were roasted alive. Then the Venetians and Constable Bourbon swung in together against the foe. Francis and his cavalry made a final charge. The Swiss, now greatly outnumbered, began to fall back toward Milan. By noon the battle was over. The hot sun blazed down unmercifully on the wounded and the dead—fifteen thousand dead, two of the enemy to one of the French.

Francis had been in the saddle for almost twenty-eight hours. His visor was pierced, his face and hands were bleeding, but he was elated with triumph.

The great adventure was over and from the horrors of battle arose the shouts of victory, the shrill notes of the fife and the beating of drums. Before the day was done Francis had written his mother, "Not for two thousand years has there been so spirited and bloody a battle."

Word of the victory spread fast. The queen mother wept with joy at the news of her heroic, victorious Caesar.

In Rome Pope Leo spluttered with rage and fear. He knew that the French would next want Naples, and Rome was on the way to Naples.

Henry VIII of England took it hard that the young French king should be so successful. Old Ferdinand of Spain was scheming to encircle France.

In the meantime Francis, towering above all, rode at the head of the triumphant procession into Milan. Oboes, clarions, and trumpets sounded. The army, in perfect order, rode through the gates to the cheers of all, even the conquered foe. Francis with his stately bearing and his gallantry charmed everyone. As a Venetian ambassador observed, "Even if you didn't know who Francis was, you would know he was a king."

And Francis was entranced by Milan. He had never seen such beautiful buildings, richly ornamented with colored marbles, such art, and such lovely, well-dressed women. He even requested that Isabella d'Este, Duchess of Mantua, send him a doll dressed exactly, even as to the hairdo, in the latest Italian fashion for his court ladies to copy.

During the elaborate festivities following his victory, Francis' keen eye observed a great deal. He noticed the elegant manners of the Italians. He also noticed something more important: their pride in their scholars and artists. He realized that France had much to learn. And in his mind he fashioned lovely palaces, full of art treasures, surrounded by gardens and fountains. He had the luck to meet Leonardo da Vinci and persuaded him to come to France as court painter. He also bought some of Leonardo's great paintings, with which he later started the famous Louvre Museum in Paris. Even today crowds gaze with wonder at Leonardo's *Mona Lisa* and *The Virgin of the Rocks*. This contact with the Italian

An Italian lady, dressed in the latest fashion which Francis wanted his court ladies to copy.

NATIONAL GALLERY OF ART, WASHINGTON

Renaissance, not his bloody battle at Marignano, was Francis' real victory.

Though Francis was immersed in festivities and delighted by Italy's beauty he also had his wits about him. He managed to make a lasting peace, known as the Perpetual Peace, with the Swiss. The Swiss had been impressed by Francis' bravery and his well-equipped army. They may have realized that France's turn had come, that Italy's day was over. This Perpetual Peace promised Swiss help to France in any future war. Strangely enough, the agreement was kept and lasted until modern times.

Pope Leo was willing to agree to almost any terms as long as the French would go no farther into Italy than Milan. He signed an agreement which gave the King of France almost complete control of the French Church, making it independent of Rome except for yearly payments.

On their return to France the conquering heroes were hailed with enthusiasm at every step. Francis' popularity was at its peak. His heroism in battle, his elegance and taste gave France a leader to be proud of. The people were willing to pay taxes for this king, they were glad to be submissive. Even *parlement,* the high court of justice, had to bow to the king who now became all-powerful. His word was law.

Fresh with ideas from Italy, Francis gave vent to his enthusiasm for building. He undertook to transform an old hunting lodge at Chambord, not far from Amboise and Chinon, into a magnificent palace. He wanted the elegance, grace, and comfort of Italian buildings. He used Italian architects and the engineering ability of Leonardo da Vinci to divert a small river to flow by the palace. But he used French stonecutters and masons, and as the château of Chambord rose higher and higher it became more and more French and less and less Italian. With its three hundred and sixty-five turrets and pinnacles, roofed in blue-gray slate, it had a grace and delicacy which were purely French. It was a far cry from the medieval, massive fortresses such as Chinon. It was designed for beauty, comfort, and luxury, not for protection. Its white stone, topped by many turrets, gave it a fairylike quality, different from the more classical marble buildings of Italy. The Italian influence showed more in the decoration than in the basic construction of the building. Intricate staircases and balconies with ornate carvings, spacious courtyards and gardens with elaborate fountains, bore the imprint of the Italian Renaissance. Within the main building was a vast stairway going up three flights. This was a double, spiral staircase where those going up could not see those going down. From balconies and terraces on the roof, ladies of the court could watch tournaments in the courtyard below or see the men coming home from the hunt. The huge park and hunting forests of Chambord covered more space than the city of Paris.

Today along the lovely, lush valley of the Loire River, Chambord and the other châteaux, like jewels dotting the landscape, still express Francis' love of beauty and the spirit of the French Renaissance.

Francis was a patron of scholars and artists as well as of architecture. With the help of his sister and a famous scholar, Budé, he founded the Collège de France in Paris. This was a refuge for true

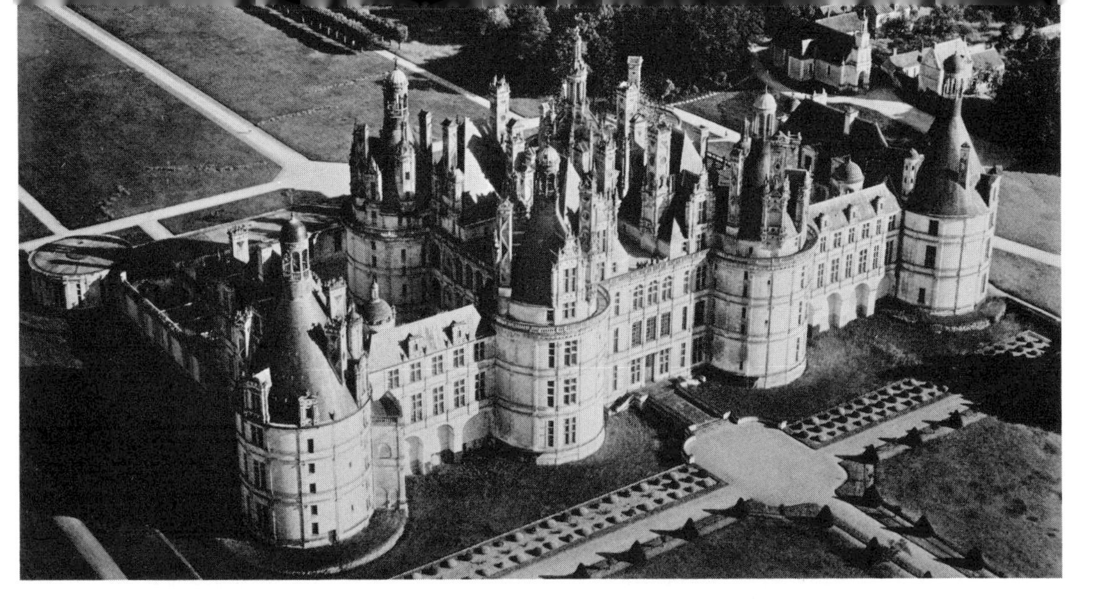

Chambord, Francis' luxurious "hunting lodge."

FRENCH GOVERNMENT TOURIST OFFICE

scholars and free thinkers where Greek, Latin, Hebrew and mathematics were taught. The king had a hard time establishing this college, for conservative churchmen disapproved of the new learning, especially the pagan Greek literature. They did their best to oppose it.

Though Francis was not a great scholar himself, he was interested in and tolerant of new ideas in education, art, and science. In fact he was the most tolerant monarch of his age. He encouraged poetry and enjoyed the company of the court poet, Clément Marot, who dared to poke fun at the church. He laughed at the stories of Dr. Francis Rabelais who poked fun at everything. Most of all he liked to talk to Leonardo da Vinci whom he regarded as a great philosopher as well as the greatest artist in the world.

While Francis was encouraging these Renaissance ideas and developing the splendor of his court, his neighbors were watching him carefully and jealously. When Ferdinand of Spain died in 1516, his grandson Charles became king of Spain. Charles was also the grandson of Emperor Maximilian of Germany and inherited vast lands from his two grandfathers.

There was a good chance that this young man would become the Holy Roman Emperor. The Holy Roman Empire had not been of much importance since the time of Charlemagne, in 800. Nevertheless, it had continued to exist and to assert its power from time to time. Most of the Germanic lands were under its sovereignty. Should Charles become emperor he would add Spain and its far-flung possessions to this Holy Roman Empire. France would really be hemmed in.

Charles, a few years younger than Francis, did not have the dash or regal bearing of the French king. Slight and unprepossessing, he had a protruding chin, a sallow complexion, and dull but determined eyes. He was serious and quiet, not caring for the ostentatious and lavish ways of a Renaissance prince. But he inherited Ferdinand's craftiness. He was clever and ambitious.

The office of Holy Roman Emperor was elective, not hereditary. In 1519 the election of a new emperor became the concern of all Europe, for each nation worried about the increasing power of other nations.

Spain, France, and England were the most concerned. Francis, overflowing with self-confidence, decided to enter the competition. Counting on his popularity, Francis dreamed of the vast empire he would have. Henry VIII of England soon backed out of the competition, and while openly pledging to support Francis he secretly helped Charles.

There were seven electors to vote for the new emperor. Unfortunately, force and fraud were often the means to success in those days. Not only the electors but all Europe became involved in the election. It was a squalid affair, each side using intimidation, deceit, and above all bribery.

The electors were pulled this way and that way as bribe after bribe increased. Francis was sure he had most of the electors on his side. He had good spies and plenty of gold. His bribes were exorbitant. But Charles managed to bribe more. In 1519 he was unanimously elected Charles V, Holy Roman Emperor. The electors went home happy, their pockets bulging with money.

This was the first rebuff that Francis had encountered and he took it hard although he tried to drown his disappointment in gaiety. Charles, with his vast empire, was now more powerful than he. Francis arranged a meeting with Henry VIII to try to cement friendship between France and England against this new great power.

This was a meeting of the greatest magnificence. The two young Renaissance kings, resembling each other in many ways, wanted to show off their wealth and power. Francis hoped to win Henry's support and friendship by dazzling him. Together they could hold in check the powerful enemy, Charles V.

The Field of the Cloth of Gold, as this meeting was later called, was one of the most sumptuous diplomatic gatherings ever held. It took place near Calais, the French city nearest England. The silk weavers of Tours worked day and night making tents of gold cloth. Artisans created gilded trees with green silk leaves. The best musicians were hired to play for ballets. Poets prepared poems of praise for the two monarchs.

Across the English Channel Henry VIII was preparing an equally grand show. English workmen had built a wooden and glass palace which was shipped piecemeal and reassembled near Calais. Its walls were covered with canvas, painted to look like stone. Its gateway was decorated with solid gold arrows and its

Charles V by Titian.

ALINARI-ANDERSON PHOTO

courtyard was full of fountains, some of which spouted wine. The ship in which King Henry crossed the Channel had sails of gold cloth.

Francis' own enormous tent was of gold cloth outside. Inside it was draped with blue velvet covered with golden fleurs-de-lys. Francis, in a cape of beaten gold set with diamonds and rubies, waited impatiently for the King of England. Henry, clothed in silver linen, was equally impatient, for the two kings had never met.

And when they did meet, their affectionate embraces, though not really sincere, gave a good show of warmth and friendliness. They exchanged gifts, Henry giving Francis a jeweled collar and Francis giving Henry an even more valuable bracelet. Together they watched pageants and tournaments. Henry was particularly impressed with the elegantly dressed and accomplished ladies of the French court.

Once while together in the royal French tent, Henry playfully suggested that he and Francis wrestle. At first Henry got the stronger grip on Francis but the French king knew this art well. Giving Henry a sudden twist, he hurled the English king to the ground. A flash of anger spread over Henry's face. He would not forget this insult to his dignity. But on the surface the friendship continued and when the festivities came to an end the two kings embraced again, each sure that he had outshone the other.

While the kings and nobles were feasting and dancing the diplomats were arranging treaties of friendship, treaties soon to be broken.

Nothing had really been proved by this great display, only hollow promises and waste of money. If Henry's dignity had been upset in his wrestling match with Francis, Francis was more upset when he learned that his new friend and ally had been conniving all the time with Charles V. In fact, no sooner had Henry left the Field of the Cloth of Gold than he hurried to meet the Emperor Charles, to whom he offered pledges of support and even his daughter in marriage. Such were treaties of friendship and alliance in those days, often made but rarely kept. Honor was much talked of but seldom heeded.

Emperor Charles, not content with the vast lands he held—all the German principalities, Spain and its overseas territory, and southern Italy—also wanted the large rich province of Burgundy, right in the heart of France. Charles's claim to Burgundy was feeble, based on the fact that his grandmother had been a Burgundian princess. His ally, Henry VIII, was talking of pressing the age-old English claim to the kingdom of France.

The powerful, wealthy constable, Charles of Bourbon, had turned traitor to France and deserted to the enemy, the emperor. Resentful that his lands had been taken over by the French crown and that his prestige had been eclipsed by the new monarch, he thought he saw a better future with the Empire.

The plan was to divide up France. The emperor would get Burgundy, Bourbon would get back his lands and more, and Henry VIII would be king of the rest of France!

The emperor started by taking Milan from the French and putting Bourbon in command. Pope Leo broke his oath of allegiance to France and joined with the enemy. It was only a decade since Francis had been the exalted hero of the battle of Marignano and had dazzled all of Europe. Yet now France was hemmed in on all sides with England, Spain, Germany, and Italy against her.

In 1524, when Francis decided to recapture Milan, it was no longer a question of a chivalrous adventure. It was now a question of holding off the formidable power of the Empire which threatened France. Milan had recently been ravaged by the plague and the imperial forces under Bourbon's command had abandoned the infested city and encamped at the nearby town of Pavia, which Francis planned to attack.

The French army was just as impressive as it had been ten years ago at Marignano. Both sides had better artillery, which had been rapidly improving. Money for this siege was again a problem but Francis stopped at nothing. More offices and titles were sold, and taxes soared. Francis even stripped St. Martin's Church of its silver and gold to buy arms.

The French assault on Pavia lasted four months. The walled town, well fortified, resisted bravely but food began to give out. The soldiers were starving and cold. They even resorted to burning the wooden beams of the church to keep warm. They ate their mules and horses to stave off starvation. It was a matter of time before they would surrender. Well fed and well supplied, the French could wait. Francis, sure of victory, even dispatched one of his detachments to Naples.

But the French did not know that Bourbon had slipped out of Pavia one night and had sped north to Germany to recruit reinforcements. Within two months he rounded up twelve thousand mercenaries. The stalemate was suddenly broken when Bourbon appeared with his new army of tough German soldiers and surrounded the unsuspecting French. Pike, lance, and arquebus confronted them on all sides.

But Francis was still sure of victory. Astride his white charger, he was magnificent in armor inlaid with gold, over which fell a cape of silver cloth. Putting on his plumed helmet with its golden salamander, he raced forward with his nobles to meet the oncoming enemy. His forces were poorly arranged and this sudden charge blocked the fire of his own artillery, rendering the superior French guns useless. Bourbon and his mercenaries pounded the French unmercifully. Many of the French nobles were killed. Francis was fighting so furiously that he did not realize that one French wing had already given way and that his Swiss pikemen were retreating. Now in the thick of the battle, Francis was wounded and bleeding. Then his horse was shot beneath him. With redoubled strength he fought on foot, amazing the enemy by his courage. Suddenly he was fighting alone, surrounded by the enemy who shouted, "It's the king, capture the king!" And Francis realized he was a prisoner. But he was a royal prisoner and even in the moment of surrender he was treated with the greatest respect. Proud Bourbon knelt before him and offered to dress his wounds.

Though dazed and crushed by this defeat, Francis maintained his regal dignity. And there was no denying he had been a great hero again. This time his letter to his mother read, "Nothing is left me save my honor and my life, which is safe."

Many of Francis' favorite nobles, heroes of Marignano, lay dead. Thousands more strewed the bloody meadows. The gates of the walled city of Pavia now burst open and the starved soldiers rushed down to pluck the booty of the fallen French.

The terms of surrender for Francis and France were harsh. Emperor Charles, delighted with Bourbon's victory for the Empire, had Francis conveyed to prison in Madrid. He demanded that Francis give him the province of Burgundy and renounce his claim to Milan; that he return to Bourbon his wealth and lands; and, finally, that he give back to England that part of France which she had claimed during the Hundred Years' War. This would have left little of France to be called France. Francis and his mother raged at such terms.

But Charles would not give an inch; he was relentless in his quest for power. For the moment Charles felt he had the world at his feet, but his vast Empire was not easy to manage. In Spain he was thought of as a German. In Germany he was considered Spanish. In Italy he was feared. He was not popular anywhere.

Francis, on the other hand, was cheered and feted as he rode through Spain on his way to prison. Though defeated, he was still a hero. Spanish ladies vied with one another to entertain him. But in prison, a prison not fit for a king, he languished and was miserable. He was not to be released until he agreed to the terms of Charles's harsh treaty, and that he refused to do. He schemed and plotted how to escape. He even sent his ring to the Turkish sultan with hope of help from the infidel Turks.

In France the queen mother did her best to run the government. She made an alliance with the new Pope Clement VII and bribed Henry VIII to join France against this powerful young Emperor Charles. Again the sides were shifting.

Finally Francis agreed to sign the Treaty of Madrid. But he had no intention of keeping it. He could later say he signed under

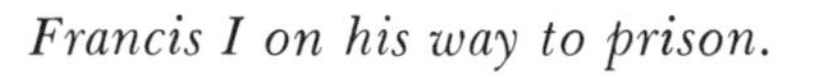

Francis I on his way to prison.

protest, against his will. Charles, suspicious of his royal prisoner, angry at the Pope and Henry VIII for shifting sides, further demanded Francis' two sons as hostages. They were to be exchanged as a pledge for Francis' oath and were to be imprisoned in exchange for Francis' freedom.

In the spring of 1525 Francis was free. Halfway across the inlet, at the frontier of Spain and France, his boat paused to greet a French boat coming the other way. This boat was bearing his sons, Francis and Henry. Francis tenderly embraced them, shed a few tears, and bade them farewell. They then exchanged boats. Francis was borne back to France and freedom. The Spanish boat turned south, taking the bewildered princes to dreary confinement in Spain.

On French soil Francis leaped onto a horse. His nerves tingled with excitement. "Now I am a king again," he shouted as he galloped north.

All France cheered to have their king home again and France agreed that the Treaty of Madrid should not be honored. Even Pope Clement absolved Francis for breaking his oath. The Pope wanted France's help against the menacing power of Charles's Empire.

Though Francis would never give up his desire for Milan he had other things to think of at the moment. He had to raise enormous sums to pay for England's friendship and his sons' ransom. He had to attend to building palaces and he had to have some fun after his dreary imprisonment. For a while he lost himself in the pleasures of court life.

The traitor Bourbon, who had been left in charge of Milan, was finding the emperor as hard to deal with as Francis. His lands and wealth had not been restored and he had not even been given enough money to pay his German and Spanish mercenaries. In the plague-ridden city of Milan, his soldiers were sick, hungry, and bloodthirsty. They wanted food and money. They thought of Rome and its riches. Desperate with this wild and uncontrollable rabble in arms, Bourbon promised them pay in Rome: "I will make you all rich or die in the attempt."

In Rome the Pope quaked with fear, for news of this oncoming army of hungry, bloodthirsty men had spread fast through the ravaged villages. The Pope shut himself up in the old fortified Castel Sant' Angelo. The attack began at dawn but just as Bourbon was starting up a scaling ladder a bullet struck him. The famous goldsmith Cellini claimed to have fired the shot. Proud Bourbon crumpled and fell beneath the trampling of his soldiers' feet. Far from home, the traitor died, a prince without a country. The leaderless troops surged over the walls and stormed the city. Plundering, murdering, destroying sacred relics and statues, mutilating churches, this horde of undisciplined imperial soldiers sacked the Holy City with as much violence as any barbarians of the Dark Ages.

All Europe was shocked at the sack of Rome and Emperor Charles had a hard time excusing the behavior of Bourbon and the imperial forces. Nevertheless Charles kept Pope Clement imprisoned in the Castel Sant' Angelo for months. The Pope's cries for help went unheeded. Finally, broken and humiliated, he escaped to his ruined palace in Orvieto. Cellini the goldsmith helped him, sewing the papal jewels into the linings of his gown. Dressed as a huckster, wearing a broad-brimmed hat, the despairing Pope left the fortress in a wagon. A few Italian statesmen such as Machiavelli deplored the sad state of Italy and feared the German-Spanish rule of Emperor Charles as a fate worse than death. Machiavelli referred to the Spanish as "wild beasts who have only the faces and voices of men."

But the inflexible Charles was still angry at the Pope's alliance with France and was enraged at Francis' dishonorable conduct in breaking the Treaty of Madrid. He ordered a harsher confinement for the little princes.

The tension between the two rivals, the Holy Roman Emperor and the Most Christian King of France, continued. But Pavia had been a turning point; the worst of the war was over. Though Francis did not realize it, Milan was lost to France forever.

If Francis had not been so obsessed with Milan and his rival, Charles V, he might have concentrated on expansion in the New

World. This would have been more profitable for France. Francis did, nowever, start French exploration in the New World. When he learned of the Pope's decree making the line of demarcation which divided the newly discovered Western lands between Spain and Portugal he was indignant. "By what right do they monopolize the world? I should like to see Adam's will and how he divided the earth." In 1524 he sent a Florentine, Giovanni Verrazano, to explore north of the Spanish possessions, to claim any land he found for France. Verrazano was also to look for a northwest passage to India. In his exploration along the North Atlantic coast, from the Carolinas to Maine, Verrazano was particularly impressed by a deep safe harbor. This was the harbor of New York and Verrazano was probably the first European to see it. He remarked that "it was not without properties of value." Though he claimed what land he saw for France, it was not until 1534, when Francis sent Jacques Cartier to look for gold and a northwest passage, that France became interested in using the new land for settlement and trade. Francis persuaded Pope Clement that occupation and settlement of new lands, not just the discovery of them, should be the basis of ownership. This was the beginning of international law and rights of ownership in overseas lands. Cartier did not find gold or a northwest passage but he found fertile land, lush fruits, abundant game and fish. He explored the St. Lawrence River, founding Mount Royal (now Montreal) and claiming Canada for France. Cartier and his men were rugged and could take the rigors of the cold winters in Canada. They also made friends with the Indians and paved the way for future French colonization.

In 1530, Francis' sons, in exchange for a huge ransom, were returned to France. They both showed signs of their long, five-year imprisonment. Young Henry was especially dark and brooding. He seldom smiled and people said he had become Spanish in prison. At this time Francis' mother died, leaving the king without his greatest prop. His sister, Marguerite, was far away in Navarre. Francis was somewhat lost without these two intelligent women to guide him.

But he did not need their guidance for his great enthusiasm for

Fontainebleau, Francis' favorite chateau in his old age.

THE METROPOLITAN MUSEUM OF ART, DICK FUND, 1930

building and beautifying France. Francis instinctively responded to beauty and admired art above all else. He once said, "I can make an army but only God can make an artist."

Francis had the ancient moated fortress of the Louvre torn down and replaced by a Renaissance palace which still stands and is now a museum, the most famous in the world.

Nearer to Paris than the châteaux of the Loire River was the old royal hunting lodge, Fontainebleau. Like the Louvre, Fontainebleau dated back to early medieval times. Francis was tired of Chambord; he wanted something even grander and he wanted a country palace suitable for his vast court, close to Paris. Francis hired a whole school of Italian architects and artists to create this most luxurious of all his palaces. It became Francis' favorite in his declining years. One can still see the Francis I gallery with its frescoed walls, carved ceilings, ornate stairways, and sculptured fireplaces. It glittered and sparkled. Statues of gods and goddesses, nymphs and fauns peered out from corners or adorned the archways. More than any other of his palaces, Fontainebleau showed the influence of the Italian Renaissance. The vast gardens and artificial pools, full of sculptured fountains, lent a watery enchantment. But the size and grandeur of this palace deprived it of the delicate beauty of the châteaux of the Loire.

Among the school of Italian artists installed at Fontainebleau was the Florentine goldsmith, Cellini, who created statues and small works of art for the king. His famous gold salt cellar was a gem of craftsmanship. The great Venetian painter, Titian, came to Fontainebleau where he probably painted his famous portrait of Francis.

French artists and architects gathered there for lavish entertainment. Budé, court librarian and founder of the Collège de France, moved the royal library from Paris to Fontainebleau. Fontainebleau became a haven for scholars, poets, artists, and ambassadors, and Francis gloried in being surrounded by such a Renaissance elite.

As Francis grew old his body was gnawed by disease. The war with Charles V went on fitfully but Francis' heart was not in it, and neither side had enough money to wage war on a large scale. France was beginning to feel the effects of expensive battles and Francis' luxurious court life. Toward the end of his life Francis lost some of his popularity but in general the people were still submissive to their absolute monarch. They seemed willing to forgive the king his extravagant ways because of his love of beauty.

In 1547, Francis learned of Henry VIII's death. A few months later Francis himself was dying. He called his son Henry and urged him to take care of the people of France, to be a wiser king than he had been.

Francis left France almost bankrupt and still menaced by the Empire. Louis XII's words, "This great boy will ruin everything," had some truth in them. Francis' longing for power, his mania for the glory of battle, and his spendthrift ways had not helped France. But his better side, his interest in art and learning and his passion for architecture, helped create and spread the French Renaissance.

Francis was a symbol for France, a symbol not only of power but of joyous, gracious living and beautiful art. The little salamander's motto, "Victory after defeat," was the victory of the Renaissance capturing all of France after the defeat of Pavia.

FRANCIS RABELAIS

Francis Rabelais in his medical beret and gown.

High above the Vienne River perched the old fortress of Chinon. Below lay the sprawling, still medieval village by the river's edge. While Francis I was training to be a prince behind the massive walls of the castle on the hill, another boy of the same age was playing in the cobbled streets below. This was Francis Rabelais, destined to be a prince of letters as the other Francis was a prince of power and a patron of art. Both boys looked out on the same river, the same lush valley, and they both had something in common—a zest for adventure and a love of life. But their lives were very different and they would not even meet for another forty years. Francis I had stately castles, courtyards, and hunting forests for his playground. Rabelais had the cobbled streets, the big caves in the hill, and the meadows for his.

Francis Rabelais was born in 1494, the same year as King Francis. He was the son of a fairly well-to-do lawyer who owned a farm and a house in Chinon where he practiced law.

Rabelais, one of four children, spent his early youth in the town of Chinon and at his family's farm, only three miles away. From his bedroom window in the little stone farmhouse Rabelais had a fine view of the countryside, of vine-clad hills and green meadows. He could see the cows grazing and he could smell the fresh juicy grapes of his father's vineyard. There was the willow grove by the little stream where neighbors "danced to the tune of merry flutes and bagpipes." Rabelais learned the ways of farm life and knew the peasants and humble folk. He knew their interests and their superstitions, he listened to their fairy tales about giants and imps.

In the town of Chinon he observed his father, a busy country lawyer, at work. Chinon looks much the same now as it did when Rabelais lived there. The old gabled, stone houses still line the narrow winding streets. Behind the village is the rocky hill, on which the castle rises. One of Rabelais' childish delights was the Painted Cave which goes deep into the hill. Its walls were painted and wine was stored in its damp, cool recesses. Next to it was Innocent's, a pastry shop, another delight for Rabelais.

La Deveniere, a farm near Chinon, birthplace of Rabelais.

Rabelais had a great imagination and an extraordinary memory. He never forgot even the smallest detail of his youth in Chinon and its surrounding countryside. When he grew up he would be able to dig down into his memory and lift out what he wanted. He would recreate incidents, people, and places with perfect accuracy. At an early age Rabelais showed great curiosity and interest in learning, which is probably why his family sent him to a monastery school.

Monasteries, which had been seats of learning all through the Middle Ages, were still a main source of education in the early sixteenth century. The Church still offered opportunities for important careers, wealth, and security. Its training was considered a good foundation for a future job.

But monasteries still had medieval schooling. Many were old-fashioned and as yet unaffected by the "new learning" of the Renaissance. Memory rather than reasoning was emphasized and students learned to say their prayers and pieces so well that they could recite them backward as well as forward and yet not understand a word. Monastery education was in need of reform. Many of the monks were lazy and ignorant. Later Rabelais described an idle monk: "Though his eyes were on the book, his soul was in the kitchen."

In spite of Rabelais's scorn for monastic education he went on studying in monasteries, for he did not scorn the Catholic religion and he planned to become a priest.

In 1520, at the age of twenty-six, Rabelais moved to a Franciscan monastery in the small town of Fontenay-le-Comte, some fifty miles from Chinon. This too was a medieval town but it was becoming a center of culture and learning. The town swarmed with lawyers, for it was a seat of the royal courts of justice. At this monastery Rabelais met a scholarly and enlightened young monk, Pierre Amy, who was interested in the Greek classics. Rabelais, who had somehow amassed an extraordinary amount of knowledge on many subjects, as yet knew little Greek. Through Pierre Amy, who became a close friend, Rabelais plunged into the study of ancient Greek with enthusiasm. This opened up a whole new world to him and exposed him to all sorts of ideas which his previous education had denied him. He and Amy pored over Greek texts on science and philosophy. These were not easy to come by and were eagerly sought after by the new Renaissance scholars, who sometimes traveled hundreds of miles to get them. Amy had been lucky to procure a few. He and Rabelais often studied them far into the night, translating and discussing ideas of the ancients which they noticed had been wrongly interpreted during the Middle Ages.

Immersed in his studies, Rabelais was annoyed at the constant ringing of bells, summoning him to prayers, mass, or chores. He thought it "the greatest foolishness to regulate one's conduct by the tinkling of bells instead of by intelligence and common sense." He did, however, find time to master Greek, and he and his friend Amy even corresponded in Greek with the great scholar Budé, King Francis' royal librarian.

The two young monks also found time to wander to town and join a group of young men, mostly lawyers, who gathered to discuss ideas of the ancients—philosophy, medicine, and law. Rabelais immediately impressed these young men by his wide knowledge on all subjects, his gift of storytelling and wonderful sense of humor.

There is no authentic portrait of Rabelais, but he was described as tall and distinguished-looking, with a merry twinkle in his black eyes. He had a most engaging personality, natural and friendly. He smiled easily and laughed often for he believed that "to laugh is natural to man." He loved and understood all types of people and they loved and admired him. In fact his company was so prized that some of the group at Fontenay urged him to throw away his monk's sackcloth and sandals and abandon the monastery so that they could enjoy his company continuously.

In the monastery Rabelais was not so popular. He spent most of his spare time studying and his spare money on books instead of contributing to collections for the Church. Franciscan monasteries of that day were anything but intellectual. Rabelais later said mockingly, "It's a monstrous thing to see a learned monk." But the learned monk, Rabelais, was soon in trouble over the innocent pastime of reading Greek. For in 1523 the Sorbonne, a powerful group of conservative churchmen of the University of Paris, ruled that the study of Greek, a pagan literature, was irreligious and must be banned. When the Sorbonne heard that two young monks were studying Greek and discussing ideas with students outside the monastery, they ordered Rabelais and his friend Amy to be put into solitary confinement and their precious Greek books to be confiscated.

This banning of Greek was a blow to the Renaissance in France. There is always a conservative group in any age which cannot bear change or new ideas. Such was the Sorbonne, which clung to the past, fearing anything new. The Sorbonnists feared that those who read the classics might turn pagan and that the Renaissance scholars who were probing into everything might upset the very foundations of Christianity. The Sorbonne became a censor, dictating what people should and should not read.

King Francis was indignant at this attempt to suppress Greek and crush the enthusiasm for the new learning. Finally through royal influence the confiscated books were returned to Rabelais and Amy. But both had begun to think the Franciscan monastery too narrow for their tastes. Amy left for Orléans and Rabelais, with papal permission, moved to a freer and more intellectual Benedictine monastery. This brush with the Sorbonne, however, was just the beginning of a lifelong duel between the Sorbonnists and the young monk, who now became a priest.

Rabelais was lucky, for the head of the Benedictine monastery, Bishop d'Estissac, was a typical Renaissance churchman. Appointed by the king, he was scholarly and cultured, with broad interests. D'Estissac was immediately attracted by the young priest and soon installed him in his home as a secretary.

Here Rabelais began a different life from the one he had known in Chinon and Fontenay. Now he sampled a freer and more aristocratic existence in which he met worldly noblemen, patrons of art, and poets of distinction. The bishop, like many wealthy churchmen of his day, was always rebuilding or adding to churches in his bishopric, and he was building a Renaissance château for himself. He traveled a great deal, checking on his buildings and various churches, and Rabelais went with him. During the four years that Rabelais spent with D'Estissac he picked up a great deal of information on architecture, law, and customs of the people. Though living among aristocrats, Rabelais found time to mingle with all sorts of people. He mixed with crowds at fairs, watched their plays, and learned what made them laugh.

The most important city of this district was Poitiers, famous for its university of law, where Rabelais may have studied. At least he became thoroughly acquainted with law, the lives of law students, and the procedure of courts of justice. Like the Church, the practice of law then was in need of reform. Lawsuits were unnecessarily long drawn out, lawyers stooped to bribes, law courts were corrupt and unjust. And the law jargon then, as now, was extraordinarily complicated with legal words and phrases which a layman could not understand.

In one of Rabelais' books he poked fun at the practice of law through an imaginary character, Judge Bridlegoose. When questioned as to how he decided cases, the old judge answered, "By the throw of my dice." He explained that he had two sets of dice, one big and one small. He used the big dice for simple cases, for they were easier to read. He used the small dice for difficult cases, for they were harder to read. He further explained that he piled all the papers for the accused on one end of his bench, all those for the accuser on the other end. When asked why he bothered to stack all these papers on his bench when a throw of the dice could decide the case right away, old Judge Bridlegoose said that the papers served him in three ways. "Firstly, for the sake of formality without which whatever is done is of no value. Secondly, they serve as a dignified and salutary form of exercise, for there is no more beneficial exercise than piling up papers, leafing through them, and turning them over. And thirdly, to take time. I am mindful that time ripens all things. I suspend, prolong, delay, and defer judgment so that the case, having been aired, sifted, and tossed to and fro, will have time to ripen and come to maturity." So Rabelais suggested that cases might be better decided by the throw of dice than by the long-drawn-out and obscure methods used by lawyers.

In 1527, Rabelais left his friend and benefactor, Bishop d'Estissac, and wandered from one university town to another. The universities then, like our graduate schools today, offered courses in theology, law, medicine, and the arts. Rabelais studied the first three. Some of the universities were good and some poor. None as yet offered the study of the classics or science. These new Renaissance interests had to be pursued by scholars on their own, outside the universities.

At the University of Orléans, Rabelais discovered that the students learned, if nothing else, to dance well and play good tennis. Orléans boasted having forty tennis courts. Tennis had been played in the Middle Ages and it became increasingly popular during the Renaissance. It had originally been a sort of handball, played first with bare hands, then with stiff gloves. Early in the sixteenth century racquets came into use, some square, some round. They were covered with parchment, which often broke. String, then gut, finally was used. Tennis nets were dangling fringes which caused frequent arguments as to whether the ball had gone over or under them.

From Orléans, Rabelais went to Paris. It was undoubtedly this big metropolis, "patched up of all nations and all manner of men," that Rabelais was most curious to see. It was a dirty, noisy place. The smell of mud and filth in the streets was overpowering. The noise of street vendors shouting their wares, the constant ringing of church and college bells were deafening. People traveled on foot

Bridge over Seine to the Left Bank.

or by mule, though there were a few coaches for the nobility. Begging monks, pilgrims, sellers of holy relics, and news vendors thronged the narrow cobblestone streets. Public fountains, only sixteen of them, provided drinking water for the entire city. Hired by the well-to-do, porters loaded down with heavy kegs of water pushed their way through the crowds.

Good smells mingled with the bad. On almost every street corner the aroma of fresh bread and pastry issued from a bakeshop. When Rabelais later visited Florence and was viewing its lovely marble buildings, he was overcome with homesickness for the smells of good French food. "These marbles are all very well, I won't deny it, but for my mind our cheese cakes are far better."

The Notre Dame bridge, newly rebuilt in the Renaissance style with Italian decoration, led over the Seine River to the Left Bank. This quarter of the city, then as now, swarmed with students, for the Left Bank was the seat of the University of Paris and its various colleges. Here was the famous Sorbonne College whose walls resounded with the noise of debates and theological wranglings.

Students, after long hours of study and harsh discipline, were often rowdy and got into frequent scrapes with the law. They had to get up at dawn, for classes started at six and continued until supper. Mealtimes were the only relaxation from study. Education at the universities, as in the monasteries, was oral. Teachers lectured and students memorized what they heard and repeated it back. Inquiring minds and experimentation were frowned upon. The Sorbonne's influence spread to all colleges in Paris and tried to stifle free thought. Rabelais felt that much time was wasted in a lot of mumbo-jumbo repetition of meaningless words.

Living conditions were poor in many of the colleges in Paris. In one, food was so bad that it was unusual not to be served rotten eggs. Rooms were so filthy that many students got ill, some died, and all contracted lice. Discipline was rigorous, with frequent floggings. "The galley slaves are far better used—the murderers in the criminal dungeons, yea, the very dogs in your house, than are the poor wretched students in this college. And if I were king of Paris, the devil take me if I would not set it on fire."

Yet in spite of such conditions in some colleges, and in spite of their narrow curricula, they were well attended, for they offered degrees in law, theology, and medicine. But no wonder that curious, eager students were driven to pursue the new interests of the Renaissance outside of the universities.

Rabelais was not young when he decided that his real interest was medicine. In 1530, at the age of thirty-six, he enrolled as a student of medicine at the University of Montpellier, in southern France. This was one of the best universities, renowned for its medical education. Through his Greek studies Rabelais had become interested in medicine and anatomy. He must have acquired a great deal of medical knowledge before he came to Montpellier, for he took examinations and got a degree after being there only six weeks. Using original Greek and Latin texts on medicine, Rabelais pointed out to fellow students the many errors of medieval medical knowledge. He, like other Renaissance scholars, had an obsession to get back to original sources on science and medicine. They were better and clearer than most medieval texts. But Rabelais also realized that knowledge of medicine through books was not enough, that doctors must also experiment to find out more about the human body.

People of that day knew little about anatomy. Leonardo da Vinci had dissected human bodies but it was still difficult to get hold of corpses for dissection. The Church thought it sacrilegious. A recently hanged criminal was sometimes procured. Occasionally, medical students, eager to learn more about anatomy, went to great lengths to get corpses, even digging up graves in the middle of the night.

Rabelais was one of the first doctors in France to give a public demonstration of dissection. Using the corpse of a recently hanged criminal and assisted by a barber-surgeon, he lectured on the various parts of the body, explaining their functions. He held his audience spellbound for hours.

The causes and cures of disease interested Rabelais and he saw the relationship between unhappiness and sickness. He realized that man alone, of all animals, is capable of laughter and that

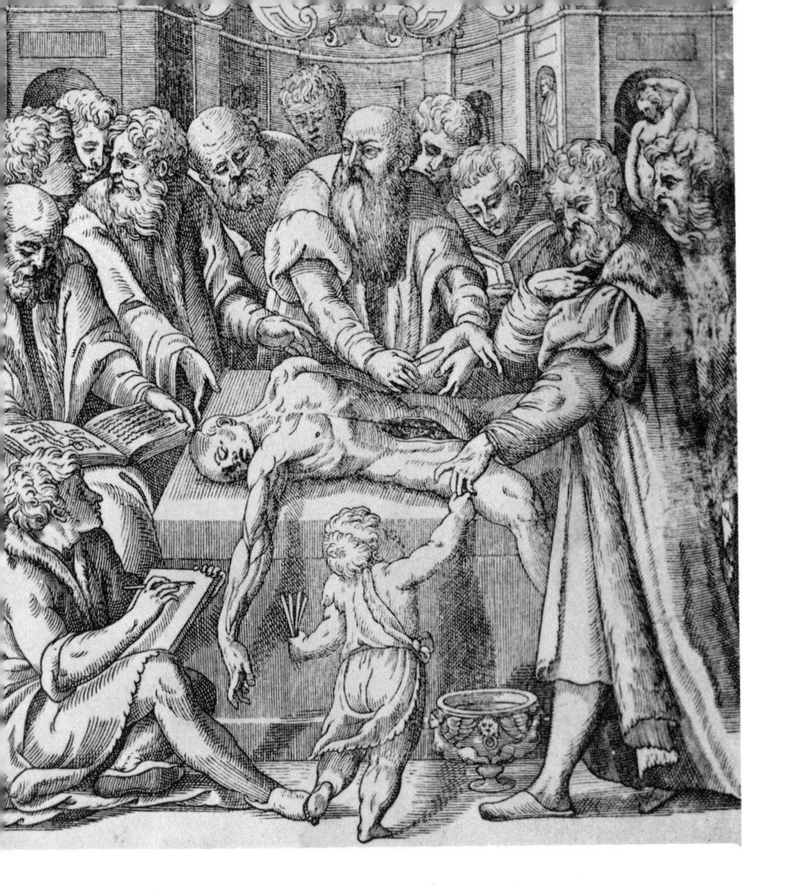

A physician lectures on anatomy.

NEW YORK ACADEMY OF MEDICINE

laughter and joy could cure some illnesses. He felt that a doctor should be comforting and gay rather than gloomy and pessimistic. He also believed that, with patience, nature cures many ills. He believed in a simple diet which would satisfy one's hunger, "though a lot of addlepated, blockhead physicians advise to the contrary." He felt that many doctors prescribed nonsensical diets and that some doctors were worse for the patient than the disease they tried to cure. And sometimes they were more interested in their fees than their cures.

Though students worked hard at this university they also had time for fun. On holidays and at graduation, banquets were given. These were followed by dancing in the streets to the light of torches and the serenading of friends with tambourines, fifes, and oboes. Plays were a frequent diversion and Rabelais took part in some of the comic ones, full of medical jokes and broad humor.

In 1532, Rabelais was on the move again. No one knows why he left Montpellier. It was probably his restless spirit, seeking more adventure. He moved to Lyons, then the intellectual center of

France. It was a freer, more tolerant city than Paris, farther away from the meddling, intolerant Sorbonne. Situated at the juncture of the Rhône and Saône rivers, Lyons was one of the crossroads of Europe and a steppingstone to Italy.

One of Lyons's chief attractions was its fairs, held four times a year. It is not surprising that printing flourished there, for books, particularly the new printed ones, were popular items at these fairs. Scholars came from all over Europe just to buy these books and Lyons became the most important center of printing and bookselling in France.

Printers' shops were confined to one section of the city and here "millions of black teeth," as the new movable type was called, often worked day and night. These shops were busy, lively places where scholars gathered to discuss new books and new ideas. The printers worked hard and seriously. In those days the printer was the publisher and bookseller as well. He was usually a scholar too, and took great pride in his finished book, treating it as a work of art. Over the door of one printer's shop was written, "Whosoever thou art, thou art earnestly requested to state thy case briefly and to take thy departure promptly for this is a place of work." Even King Francis was kept waiting in a printer's shop while the printer finished correcting a proof.

Rabelais, already known for his excellent Greek and knowledge of law and medicine, was immediately sought by the printers. He was asked to translate Greek texts on medicine and anatomy. Some of these were published and his fame spread.

Rabelais had not been in Lyons long before he was asked to be chief physician and lecturer on medicine at the hospital, Hôtel de Dieu. This was considered an up-to-date hospital even though two or three patients had to share one bed! But they did have clean white linen sheets, for Rabelais was particular about hygiene. The patients, about one hundred and fifty, were in a large hall, men on one side, women on the other. At one end was a chapel and at the other a huge fireplace, the only source of heat. A separate room was provided for contagious diseases. Sixteen nurses, an apothecary, a barber-surgeon, and a chaplain made up the staff. Rabelais, the

L'Hotel de Dieu, a hospital of Rabelais' time.

THE METROPOLITAN MUSEUM OF ART, NEW YORK

physician, made daily rounds with his staff. He advised the barber-surgeon and the apothecary on treatment and cures. Soon after he was installed the death rate fell considerably, and Rabelais' reputation as an excellent doctor became known far and wide. He was greatly loved by his patients for his sympathy, his sense of fun, and his good common sense.

Though he was now a busy doctor, he found time to pursue his other interests. Famous scholars dropped in to see him almost every day, for it was considered a privilege to talk and listen to the great physician.

He achieved eminence as a scholar and physician, but never lost touch with the common people. He had read old tales about giants, published in cheap pamphlet form for the amusement and diversion of simple folk. When *The Most Horrific Life of the Great Gargantua* and *Pantagruel, King of the Dipsodes, with His Heroic Acts and Prowesses* came off the printing press, everyone recognized beloved characters of old fairy tales which were part of medieval folklore, and soon everyone knew that the author, Dr. Alcofribas Nasier was really Dr. François Rabelais (for his pen name is his own, scrambled).

No one knows when he found the time to write these as well as medical treatises, but he mentions writing at mealtimes and late at night.

Rabelais' Gargantua was a Renaissance giant with an enormous appetite for adventure, knowledge, and experience. The very name "Gargantua" now means big, and it took "seventeen thousand nine hundred and thirteen cows" to supply milk for this huge baby giant. It took "nine hundred yards of linen to make him a shirt." Pantagruel, his son, had a certain "jollity of mind" and was a wise and reasonable giant, benefiting from the new Renaissance education. If Gargantua had a great appetite, Pantagruel had an enormous thirst for all knowledge and experience. These tales were the first part of Rabelais's great literary work. They were immediately popular with everyone except the Sorbonne. As soon as that conservative body heard about them, they were condemned. But the Sorbonne could not suppress the books themselves and the printers had a hard time keeping up with the popular demand.

They became best sellers because Rabelais used well-known themes and everyday language—language used by the common people, natural and sometimes even gross. Through his giants, Rabelais wove stories so true to life, so full of the spirit of the times, that they have been called the mirror of the Renaissance. They appealed to the common man, for he saw his own life acted out by giants. They appealed to scholars for their extraordinary erudition and knowledge on all subjects. And finally they appealed to almost everyone, whether high- or low-born, for their delightful, rollicking humor.

It was this humor that the Sorbonne did not like, for it was often at the expense of narrow-minded, intolerant groups like the Sorbonne. Though never in a bitter, sarcastic way, Rabelais poked fun at many things: the old narrow education, lazy monks, war, medieval medicine, superstition, the injustice of law, and above all intolerance. And the Sorbonnists, who used long, pedantic phrases, were ridiculed: "A plague upon these windbags who stifle an idea to death under a blanket of words." Far from the spirit of the Sorbonne was Rabelais' ideal education, which he described at the end of his first book. His delightfully free and undisciplined school, the Abbey of Thélème (from the Greek word meaning desire), was as opposite as possible from the monastery schools of that time. The one rule to be observed was, *"Fais ce que vouldras,"* or "Do as you like."

Abbey of Thélème, showing its grand staircase and the inscription, "Fais Ce-que Vouldras" or "do as you like."

In planning the layout of the school, first of all was discussed what there would *not* be. It was agreed there should be no walls around this school, for walls (*murs* in French) cause murmurs or whisperings. There would be no clocks or bells, for as Gargantua said, "The greatest loss of time is to watch the hands of the clock and conduct oneself by the tinkling of bells." And over the gateway was inscribed who were not welcome: hypocrites, bigots, money-grabbing lawyers, liars, cowards, cheaters, lazy slugs, or ugly thieves. Those who were welcome were lovely young girls between the ages of ten and fifteen and handsome young men between the ages of twelve and eighteen, all who were pure, honest, and wise. "For those who are free and well brought up are naturally drawn toward virtue and withdrawn from vice." Rabelais believed that freedom encouraged virtue and suppression encouraged vice.

The school itself was so accurately described that architects have even made models of it. It was a hundred times more magnificent than King Francis' palace of Chambord. It had six stories and nine thousand three hundred and thirty-two rooms! It was a delightfully exaggerated Renaissance palace with every conceivable luxury, including swimming pools and a theater. Tennis courts, tilting grounds, gardens, orchards with all kinds of fruit trees, and a large park full of wild game surrounded it.

Students in this paradise of do-as-you-like schooling were free and happy. With no rules to bother them they became so well educated that there was not one who could not read, write, sing, play musical instruments, and speak five or six languages. They were well-rounded Renaissance ladies and gentlemen, skilled in mind and body, free to pursue all that life could offer.

All this the Sorbonne would not tolerate and some of it they could not understand. That made them angrier than ever.

Rabelais had been helped in his first brush with the Sorbonne by his benefactor, D'Estissac. Now he luckily met another, even more influential Renaissance churchman who came to his aid and protection. This was Cardinal Jean du Bellay, scholar and diplomat. The cardinal took a great liking to the doctor, admiring his medical skill and enjoying his delightful companionship. Possibly to help Rabelais avoid the wrath of the Sorbonne, Du Bellay took him as his personal physician on a diplomatic errand to Rome.

Even King Francis did his best to protect Rabelais from persecution by the Sorbonne, for the king admired "The Book," as Rabelais' tales were now called, so much that he had it read aloud constantly.

But in the fall of 1534 an unfortunate incident, which became known as the Affair of the Placards, made the tolerant King Francis change his attitude. One night fanatical critics of the Church posted anti-Catholic placards on public buildings throughout the country. In vile and abusive language these placards attacked the Pope, mass, and many other sacred rituals. These extremists even dared to post a placard on the king's bedchamber door. Francis was shocked and angry. He also feared an uprising and he, who had fought the intolerance of the Sorbonne, now gave it full power to censor and persecute as it saw fit. It was a dark time for religious reformers and Renaissance scholars. The Sorbonne failed to distinguish between the two, and persecuted innocent scholars as well as anti-Catholics. Many were burned at the stake.

Rabelais did not have to worry about the success of his books. The more they were condemned the more they sold. But he did have to worry about his life. He had seen someone burned at the stake and did not want to share the same fate. In his book he mentions a town where "they are burning their regents alive like red herrings," and his giant Pantagruel, voicing Rabelais' thoughts, said, "I hope I never die like that. I am naturally quite thirsty enough without being heated any more."

Many Renaissance scholars, fearing persecution, hid their Greek books and stopped criticizing or poking fun at anything that would offend the Sorbonne. Others like Rabelais simply disappeared.

By the spring of 1535 the persecution had died down and Rabelais returned to Lyons. His benefactor, Du Bellay, was off to Rome once more and again asked Rabelais to go along as his physician. On his first trip to Rome Rabelais had been absorbed in its antiquity and its ancient ruins. This time he was more interested in the everyday life. "At Rome," he wrote, "a world of folks gets an honest livelihood by poisoning, drubbing, lambasting, stabbing, and murdering." Such was Rome then, full of intrigue, plots, and murders. On this trip Rabelais had a chance to attend to something which must have weighed on his mind, particularly during the past year of the Sorbonne's persecution. Through the influence of Du

A burning at the stake such as Rabelais hoped to avoid.

LIBRAIRIE LAROUSSE

Bellay, he managed to get a pardon from the Pope for being a "lapsed monk." Rabelais had given up his monk's habit, without permission, when he became a doctor. He obtained approval to stay in the Benedictine order and also to practice medicine, provided he did not practice for gain. Now he could remain a priest and be a doctor too.

But it is not surprising that Rabelais lost his job at the hospital. With his frequent trips with Du Bellay and his sudden disappearances to avoid the wrath of the Sorbonne he could hardly expect to keep a steady job. His writings brought him little money, for the publisher-printer got practically all the profit in those days. Henceforth he depended on the Church and on his patrons for financial support. For the rest of his life Rabelais was a wanderer, sometimes practicing medicine, sometimes disappearing, but always writing.

Again Du Bellay's influence helped him. He was made master of the King's Requests, an honorary position, often given to poets and men of letters. This gave him the privilege of traveling with the royal court. In 1538, Rabelais was with the royal entourage at a peace meeting between the ever warring King Francis and Emperor Charles V. The Pope had arranged this meeting to bring peace to Europe and also to get the combined help of France and the Empire in stamping out the mounting revolt against the Catholic Church.

The peace treaty, as usual, had little lasting effect, and Charles V and King Francis were soon at war again. To show the folly and stupidity of these wars Rabelais invented a wonderfully silly war among his giants. Using a real life incident, a family feud between his father and a neighbor over fishing rights in the little Vienne River, flowing by Chinon, Rabelais conceived one of the greatest and certainly the funniest wars of all times, the Cake Bakers' War. This great war of enormous giants all takes place in the quiet little countryside between Chinon and Rabelais' farm.

The Cake Bakers, subjects of the giant king, Picrohole (meaning Bitterbile), were traveling along the road taking cartloads of cakes to sell at a nearby town. Some gentle shepherds, subjects of the good giant, Grangousier, thinking those cakes would be heavenly to eat, politely asked if they could buy some. The cake bakers

Gargantua demolishes Picrohole's castle.

not only refused to sell them but for no reason at all overwhelmed the shepherds with insults, calling them "lubbery louts, lazy loons, monkey faces, slabberdegullian druggles, slapsauce fellows," and other such horrible names. This of course started a fight, which the cake bakers were certainly looking for. And then their king, Picrohole, "without any inquiry or counsel or reflection," ordered the drums to beat, his banners to unfurl, and his troops to assemble. And without any military order whatsoever, his army advanced on Grangousier's land, laying waste to everything in sight. "They drove off oxen, cows, sheep, and chickens. They knocked down walnuts, picked vines clean, carried off hedges, and shook all the fruit off the trees."

The first resistance they met was at the monastery (right next to Rabelais' farm) where the most unmonkish of monks, Friar John, "gallant, bold, and frisky," put up a great fight. Seeing the enemy destroying the monastery vineyard, Friar John, armed with his staff, rushed out and slashed at the cake bakers right and left. "He beat in their heads, pushed in their noses, broke arms and legs. If any tried to hide, he squashed him flat as a flounder. If any tried to escape by climbing trees, he impaled him with his staff. Alone he slew almost all. Some died without speaking, others spoke without dying, some died speaking, others spoke dying." No one, before or since, ever fought so valiantly as Friar John.

But the good giant, Grangousier, whose land Picrohole had invaded, wanted peace, not war. He sent a message to Picrohole, reminding him of their former alliance and friendship. "What madness is it, then, that leads you, breaking off your alliance and trampling all the bonds of friendship underfoot, contrary to all lawful rights? Where is your good faith, where is reason, where is your humanity?"

Rabelais, of course, knew of the many broken treaties between Charles V and King Francis. Rabelais is serious here, pleading for reason and humanity, for peace, not war.

The wise words of giant Grangousier fell on deaf ears. Picrohole would not listen to reason and Grangousier was forced to recall his son, Gargantua, from his studies in Paris, to help defend his homeland. Armed with a huge tree for his lance, astride his enormous gray mare, Gargantua rushed toward the fortress which Picrohole had captured. "With mighty blows he overthrew both towers and fortress and laid all level with the ground." The great Cake Bakers' War came to an end.

But the real war between King Francis and the Emperor Charles continued. Francis again contemplated attacking Milan and had already captured the nearby Italian city of Turin. In 1539 he sent the younger brother of Cardinal du Bellay to govern and fortify Turin. Rabelais was asked to go along as his physician. Rabelais admired this statesman more than any man he ever met, for Governor du Bellay was the finest type of Renaissance aristocrat, thoughtful, wise, and humane. He was the inspiration for the giant Pantagruel's treatment of conquered peoples. "The manner of preserving newly conquered countries is not to oppress, vex, and devour the people but, by enticements of love, his justice will appear in the good will and affection of the people if he doth what is right to everyone." This was a far cry from the general run of rulers of those times.

Unfortunately this fine statesman died in 1542 and Rabelais was again without a job. He was not heard of until 1546 when his third book appeared. In spite of this book having royal backing, it too was condemned by the Sorbonne. Ever since the meeting between Charles V and King Francis, the Sorbonne had exercised its full power of censorship. Rabelais was discouraged and took off for the free city of Metz, just beyond the French border. Here he was free, if penniless. During his stay King Francis died and Renaissance scholars lost their most important patron and support.

Rabelais' exuberant nature could not stay discouraged for long and he finished another book, his fourth and last, by 1552. Influenced by exploration and newly discovered distant lands, Rabelais' fourth book leads us on a fantastic voyage to the Far East. It is full of adventures and delightful nonsense. The giant Pantagruel set off with a "great fleet of triremes, galleons, and feluccas, well rigged and caulked, for Cathay which lay in upper India." He took a short cut, not the long route the Portuguese used, "sailing through the torrid zone at the south point of Africa, beyond the equinoctial line, and losing sight of the Northern Pole, their guide." Pantagruel, like the French explorer, Cartier, headed for a northwest passage, "so that winding under the north, not too close for fear of being shut up in the frozen sea, they must have that on the right to the eastward, which at their departure was on their left." This sounds a bit confused as indeed the voyage was but "this proved a much shorter cut, for without shipwreck, danger, or loss of men, they performed in less than four months the voyage of Upper India, which the Portuguese, with a thousand inconveniences and innumerable dangers, can hardly complete in three years."

As Rabelais might have expected, this book was likewise condemned. It was too bad the teachers of the Sorbonne could not laugh more easily, for though this book again poked fun at them it also poked fun at their greatest enemies, the extreme Protestant reformers. Rabelais felt that these Protestants had become as narrow and intolerant as the Sorbonnists themselves. He felt that they were against all joy and fun in life and he labeled them "false zealots, deformed and made in spite of nature."

After the publication of this book it was rumored that Rabelais had been thrown into prison. In any case the great doctor and humorist vanished. The next report of him was his death in 1553. When Rabelais died the joy and exuberance of the French Renaissance were beginning to wane and France was on the eve of bloody civil wars of religion.

But Rabelais, the most original writer that France ever had, preserved for us the free and joyous spirit of the Renaissance age when man was trying out many new ideas. He did much to enrich the French language and his rapid flow of words, full of sound and rhythm, suggest another literary genius, William Shakespeare. Like Shakespeare, he used whatever material was at hand and turned the commonplace into wonderful, imaginative stories.

Rabelais was above all a humorist but beneath his humor were serious ideas. His books plead for reason and humanity, for peace, not war, for education through thinking, not just memory, for justice in law, and for love of one's neighbor.

Rabelais, like other Renaissance men, was intoxicated with the new golden age of literature and learning. A letter of his giant, Gargantua, to his son Pantagruel so well sums up the spirit of the age that it has been called the Hymn of the Renaissance. First it shows the Renaissance scorn for the past: "The time then was not for learning as it is at present. For that time was darksome, obscured with clouds of ignorance, showing the calamities brought about by the Goths who had destroyed all literature; but through divine goodness, in my own lifetime, light and dignity have been restored to the art of letters. Now all branches of science, so long extinct, have been re-established and languages have been restored to their pristine purity. Printing, now in use, is elegant and correct. The latter was invented in my own lifetime through divine inspiration just as artillery, on the other hand, was invented by the devil. The world now is full of scholarly men, learned teachers, and ample libraries—why, even women have aspired to learning."

This letter reflects the spirit of the Renaissance but it also ends with a message which is as important today as it was then: "Wisdom cannot enter an unkind soul, and since knowledge without conscience is but the ruin of the soul, serve and love God. Be of service to your neighbors and love them as yourself."

Rabelais' giants, Gargantua and Pantagruel, were Renaissance men in their eagerness to know and explore all. And if they made men laugh, they also made men think. They, like Rabelais, were reasonable and in their desire to correct abuses of the past they were constructive in their hopes for the future.

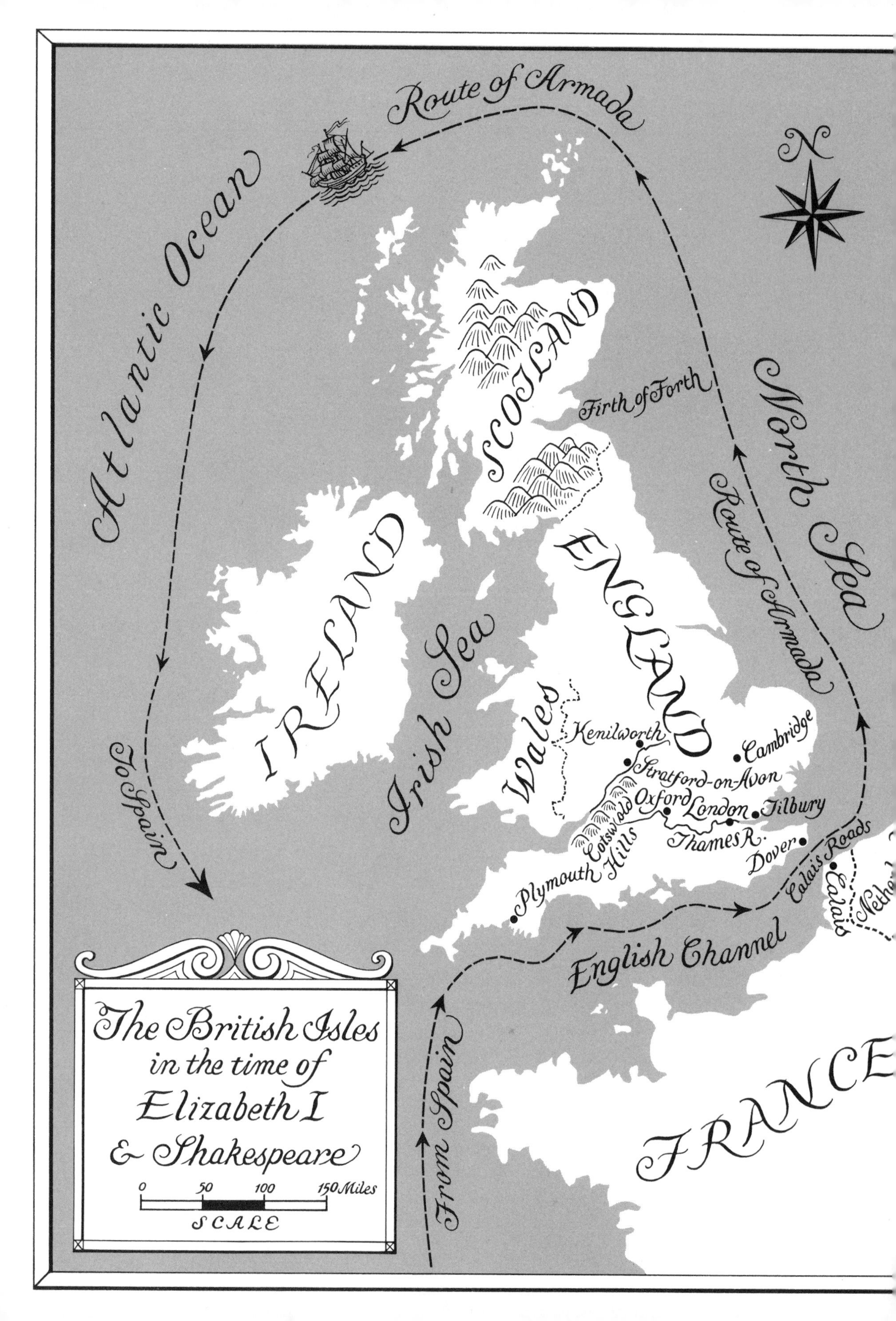
The British Isles
in the time of
Elizabeth I
& Shakespeare
0
50
100
150 Miles
SCALE
Route of Armada
Atlantic Ocean
N
SCOTLAND
Firth of Forth
North Sea
Route of Armada
IRELAND
ENGLAND
Irish Sea
Wales
Kenilworth
Stratford-on-Avon
Cambridge
Oxford
London
Tilbury
Cotswold Hills
Thames R.
Dover
Plymouth
Calais Roads
Calais
To Spain
English Channel
From Spain
FRANCE

PART 4
ENGLAND AWAKES

English countryside with stately mansion in background.

BRITISH INFORMATION SERVICES

THE British Isles lie north of France and are separated from the continent of Europe by the North Sea and the English Channel. Before Columbus' time these islands were at the outer edge of the known world though only twenty miles separate them from the Continent.

The largest of these islands, Great Britain, is divided into England, Scotland, and Wales. England, the core of the island, is a little larger than the state of New York. But England's influence in the world has been out of all proportion to her small size.

England is a lush, mellow country of green pasture land, gently rolling hills, and slow rivers. Its island weather is subject to quick changes, sudden showers, and brief sunshines. Its "meadows . . . shining in the rain" and its "sweet inland waters" have inspired poets for ages past.

To the west of England lies a harsher land. This is Wales, with mountains cut by deep green valleys and rushing streams, facing the Atlantic Ocean and the Irish Sea.

Scotland to the north is harsher still, a land of mountains lost in clouds and mists, of wild moorlands and countless islands.

Near the mouth of the wide navigable river Thames is London, an ancient city, dating back to Roman times.

It has been said that England owes her fortunes to the sea. At first the sea brought invaders who easily conquered the unfortified island—Romans, Angles and Saxons, and Normans. But after the Norman Conquest in 1066 invasions of the island ceased and England began to fortify itself from attack. The rough waters between it and the mainland of Europe became a defense and England became an island fortress.

One can read the history of England in its ancient buildings, so well preserved. The English landscape is dotted with feudal castles and Gothic cathedrals, villages of weathered stone houses, and cottages of plaster with thatched roofs and tiny rose gardens. Old Tudor houses and inns, of half timber and half brick or plaster, with upper stories overhanging, still line the streets of towns or cities. Stately Renaissance mansions or palaces of stone or red brick

Tudor houses which still line the streets of many English towns.

BRITISH INFORMATION SERVICES

with marble decoration are surrounded by formal gardens and vast deer parks.

When the Hundred Years' War with France ended in 1453, England was plunged into one last convulsive struggle before the feudal barons could be quelled and the monarchy could bring the nation under control. While Spain and France were emerging as unified, powerful nations, England still had lawless barons struggling in bloody wars against the Crown. These were known as the Wars of the Roses. In 1485 the Battle of Bosworth Field ended this baronial strife and a new king of Welsh descent, Henry Tudor, became Henry VII.

A strong monarchy was needed to subdue the rebellious nobles and set the country in order. Henry VII, like Louis XI in France, was cautious and thrifty. He chose for advisers men of ability, not nobility, and turned to the middle classes for support. He was not a colorful king, but his shrewdness and parsimony brought order and peace to England. His encouragement of trade and his building up of a merchant fleet brought prosperity. He was interested in the arts and education. He encouraged the new learning of the Renaissance which began to trickle into England.

In an attempt to broaden England's horizon he married a daughter to the king of Scotland and a son to Catherine of Aragon, the daughter of Ferdinand and Isabella.

His son Henry became King Henry VIII in 1509. Great was the rejoicing when this dashing, handsome prince was crowned. A skilled athlete, an excellent dancer and musician, Henry was also well educated and could converse in French, Italian, and Latin. He was a true Renaissance prince. With red-gold hair and powerful build, he dressed in colorful ostentation. His magnetic personality captivated his people. He wielded almost, not quite, as much power as the absolute monarch across the Channel, Francis I.

After eighteen years of married life, Henry became obsessed with the fact that Catherine had produced no son and heir—only one daughter, Mary. Besides, he was thinking that a young lady in waiting would make a more attractive wife. He appealed to the Pope for a divorce from his wife but had no success.

Angry at being balked, Henry took matters into his own hands. First, with the backing of his pliable Parliament, he cut down yearly payments to the Pope, hoping to force the Pope to give him a divorce. When that failed, he went still further and had himself made supreme head of the Church of England. He obtained his divorce through his own Archbishop of Canterbury and married his beloved Anne Boleyn.

Henry VIII of England.

NATIONAL PORTRAIT GALLERY, LONDON

This bold step shocked all Europe but it was a popular move in England. For some time there had been discontent and criticism of the wealth and corruption in the Catholic Church. Parliament supported Henry, not because it approved of his divorce, but because it approved of a break with Rome and the Pope. This was an expression of a new national feeling, that England should manage her own affairs, even church affairs. It was not a desire to change the Catholic religion, but it was a first step toward the Reformation which was already in full bloom across the Channel.

Henry now became the most powerful monarch England ever had. Parliament could have checked him, for the principle that Parliament was the ultimate authority had long since been established in England. But instead, Parliament passed an act stating that it was treason for anyone to criticize the king! The gallows were full and the sound of the executioner's ax was frequent.

It was a great disappointment to Henry when his new wife, Anne, produced another daughter. To make way for still another wife he had Anne beheaded. His third wife produced the longed-for son and heir. But before his reign was ended Henry had had a total of six wives.

Henry involved England in the futile struggles between Spain and France, seesawing back and forth with whichever side seemed most to his advantage. He wasted much of the country's wealth on such ventures but he brought back Renaissance ideas and taste from the Continent.

It is hard to see why this ruthless, selfish king was so popular. But England, shattered by the Wars of the Roses, wanted a strong monarchy. Henry's abilities and dashing elegance were admired and his ruthlessness belonged to the age. He was no worse than Ferdinand or Francis I. His break with Rome gave England a sense of national pride and independence.

His son became Edward VI. His brief reign is remembered mostly for the spread of Protestantism. The Bible, recently printed in English, became available to the people. Church services were conducted in English instead of Latin. Now able to understand the services, people took a new interest in the Church. Protestantism seemed established.

But when the crown passed to Mary, Edward's older sister, the situation was reversed. Mary, daughter of Henry and his first wife, Catherine of Aragon, had been brought up strictly by her Spanish mother in the old Catholic tradition. Her faith had been her one consolation in an unhappy childhood. Mary tried to bring England back to its traditional Catholic role and reopened relations with Rome and the Pope. This was most unpopular and when Mary married Philip of Spain, a zealous Catholic and a foreigner, the people were furious. In the name of religion Mary and Philip started a persecution of heretics that became so steeped in blood that Mary is forever remembered as Bloody Mary. Far from accomplishing what she wanted, she increased the enthusiasm for Protestant beliefs. Those who went to the stake—at least three hundred—were looked up to as saintly martyrs. The unhappy queen died knowing that all England looked forward to a change.

The break with Rome paved the way for the great flowering of England's Renaissance. It established England's independence and gave her the impetus to expand her trade overseas and to explore and conquer new lands. At home her energy burst into the greatest flowering of literature the world had ever known.

England, last of all the European countries, awoke to her full Renaissance when Elizabeth, the fragile red-haired daughter of Henry VIII, took the throne in 1558.

ELIZABETH I

Young Queen Elizabeth in her coronation robes.

RADIO TIMES HULTON PICTURE LIBRARY, LONDON

EVERYONE in England expected a prince. The physicians as well as the astrologers had predicted the birth of a son. No one dared to think of a girl after all that the King had been through to present his country with a male heir: defied the Pope, divorced his Queen Catherine and married Anne Boleyn.

On September seventh, 1533, Queen Anne was delivered of a baby girl, the future Queen Elizabeth. The king had to be told the disappointing news. It was said that King Henry's anger was such that the earth trembled. Another girl! Was it for this that he had dared so much? He still had no male heir and the proclamation, ready long ago to send to the royal courts of Europe announcing the birth of a prince, had to be hurriedly changed. There was just barely enough room to squeeze in a little "s" after the word prince to make it look more like princess.

No one felt the disgrace of this daughter more than the mother, Queen Anne. She had failed the king.

When Elizabeth was not quite three years old the king had her mother executed. Henry made one concession to his queen. He hired a skillful French headsman who used a sword instead of an ax. Assured she would feel no pain, Queen Anne approached her death with courage. "I have a little neck," she laughed, putting her hand around it and placing her head upon the block.

Elizabeth was too young to be affected by this at the time. She was in the safekeeping of a governess in a palace beyond the gates of London. Fair of skin, with the red-gold hair of her father, bright brown eyes and faint eyebrows, Elizabeth was a lively child, quick to respond and quick to learn. She was dressed lavishly in orange velvets or yellow satins. But after her mother's execution and the birth of Prince Edward her status changed. She was no longer a princess, just Lady Elizabeth. Her clothes allowance was cut and her governess complained bitterly that her clothes were outgrown, that she had nothing to wear.

By the time Henry had married a fifth wife, Catherine Howard, things had changed again. Henry's fifth wife was kindly and gay. She invited Elizabeth to join her brother, Prince Edward, at court. When Elizabeth dined in the great hall at Hampton Court she could look at the ceiling and see the initials of her father and mother, H and A, intertwined in the ornately carved woodwork. The carving had scarcely been finished before her mother's execution. And soon this queen, who was so kind to Elizabeth, was to suffer the same fate. When Elizabeth was not quite eight, Queen

Catherine Howard was beheaded on the very spot where Anne Boleyn had met her death so courageously.

In spite of such horrors in her early youth, Elizabeth adored her father. To her he was the greatest man and greatest king on earth. And in spite of a childhood which was not normal by our standards Elizabeth's youth was not completely without love and affection. She and her brother Edward became close companions and Elizabeth had a devoted governess.

Elizabeth and Edward were tutored by young men from the University of Cambridge where Protestant ideas mingled with the Renaissance learning. They studied history, geography, astronomy, and French, Italian, and Spanish. Elizabeth's special Latin and Greek tutor, Roger Ascham, found his young mistress an extraordinary pupil. "Her mind has no womanly weakness and her perseverance is equal to that of a man, and her memory long keeps what it quickly picks up," he wrote to a friend. Elizabeth's love of learning and thirst for knowledge never abated. She kept up her studies of Latin and Greek even when she became queen.

At the age of seventeen Elizabeth went to London to visit her brother Edward, the king, who was ill and had not long to live. People turned out to see the princess ride by and even then Elizabeth, pale of face, her red-gold hair tied smoothly back (unlike the frizzled style of the day), dressed in simple elegance, showed a magnetic personality which caught the people's eye.

Three years later Elizabeth rode to London in the coronation procession of her older sister, Queen Mary. Elizabeth and Mary were quite a contrast. Mary, thirty-seven, looked even older. Her unhappy youth had left its mark and her face was sallow and wrinkled. People noticed how she resembled her Spanish mother, Catherine of Aragon. She seemed to belong to the old England which was dying. Elizabeth, not quite twenty, carried her fine young figure with grace and elegance. People noticed how much she resembled her father, great King Henry VIII. She bore the stamp of the new and Protestant England. Most of the London crowds who filled the streets to watch the procession were Protestant. Mary may not then have realized that the enthusiastic shouts of the multitudes were directed more toward her younger sister than to herself.

Mary's attempt to restore Catholicism to England during her five-year reign was a sad and bloody failure. It was a sad time too for Elizabeth, who was under a cloud of suspicion. Mary knew of Elizabeth's Protestant upbringing and she suspected that Elizabeth's conformity to the Catholic religion was a pretense, as indeed it was. Elizabeth did not want to have her head chopped off. She tried to conform to Catholicism to keep peace with her sister but it was noted that she did not always attend Mass. And when a Protestant rebellion broke out Elizabeth's name was involved. The rebels hoped to overthrow Mary and put Elizabeth on the throne.

Elizabeth was ordered to London where she could be closely watched. As she and her retinue approached the city, they were confronted with a gruesome sight. Corpses of the rebel Protestants dangled from the City gateways. Severed heads adorned the public buildings. Elizabeth shuddered as she wondered what was in store for her.

And when Elizabeth found out that she was to be conveyed to the Tower of London as a prisoner, she was frantic. Many people who went into the Tower never came out. The Tower of London was not just one tower, but an old Norman castle built in 1066 by William the Conqueror. Its main keep, or White Tower, was still used for state occasions by monarchs and nobility but its many thick-walled towers, rising above the crenellated walls, served as prisons for royalty and important persons. Not far from the Tower chapel stood the execution block on which Elizabeth's mother and stepmother had been beheaded.

Elizabeth felt she must be allowed to see her sister, the queen, or at least write her a letter declaring herself innocent of any part in the rebellion. But Mary was not moved and when the river tide was right and the townsfolk were at church, for it was Palm Sunday, a barge bearing Elizabeth and her guards swept down the Thames under London Bridge, and bore her to the Tower gateway.

Tower of London. Prisoners entered by the Traitor's Gate in foreground.

FOLGER SHAKESPEARE LIBRARY, WASHINGTON

It was raining as the barge pulled into the gate—Traitor's Gate, as it was called. The portcullis with its iron grating and pointed spikes was raised to receive the royal prisoner. One of the guards offered his cloak but Elizabeth dashed it aside. She mounted the steps and walked on through the gaping archway which had led so many to torture and death. Suddenly she sat down on a damp stone and refused to go farther. "O Lord," she cried, "I never thought to have come in here as a prisoner; and I pray you, all good friends, bear me witness that I come in here no traitor but as true a woman to the queen's majesty as any now living." When one of the gentleman ushers broke down and wept, Elizabeth, scorning his weakness, rose and followed her guards to the Bell Tower, up the winding stairs to a vaulted stone room where three small Gothic windows let in a little light. The door closed behind her and her ladies in waiting.

Unable to prove anything against Elizabeth, Mary had her taken to Woodstock Castle, far removed from troublesome Protestants who might try to rescue the prisoner. Elizabeth was to be conveyed secretly by barge, then in a litter overland. But the secret leaked out and people, thinking the princess to be free, greeted her with enthusiasm. Her journey to Woodstock Castle was more like a triumphal procession than the secret journey of a prisoner. Throngs greeted her with shouts of joy at every village along the way. At least, in this hour of peril, Elizabeth knew that the people loved her.

In Woodstock, shut off from the world, Elizabeth brooded over her fate. She had to be wary, for the least mistake might send her back to the Tower and death. On a windowpane she scratched with her diamond:

> Much suspected, by me
> Nothing proved can be.

After anxious months release came unexpectedly. Elizabeth was summoned to Hampton Court. Mary and her husband, King Philip II of Spain, were holding court there and Mary was ill. Philip was anxious to meet Princess Elizabeth. Should Mary die, he felt he might have to marry Elizabeth to save England from lapsing back into Protestantism.

At Hampton Court Elizabeth came face to face with her future enemy, the Most Catholic King of Spain. Short and fair with a protruding chin, Philip cautiously eyed the slender young princess with her fiery eyes and long delicate hands. How different she was from her sister Mary!

In 1558, when Mary died, Elizabeth was just twenty-five. Tall and straight, she still looked young and fragile. But beneath her delicate form there was a harshness and firmness, shaped by years of anxiety, of watching and waiting. She had the proud disdain of her father but she had the cleverness and wisdom of her grandfather, Henry VII, too. She was a great politician, master of veiled words and phrases of double meanings which would exasperate and baffle so many rulers of Europe. But her brilliant smile, her witty conversation, her red-gold hair and snow-white skin cast a magic spell on all who met her.

England was ready for this daughter of the Renaissance as France had been ready for Francis I. Tired of past miseries and religious persecution, the English looked forward to a new reign of peace and joy and prosperity.

The day before the coronation ceremony the great coronation procession from the Tower of London through the city gates to Westminster Abbey took place. Elizabeth and her entire court, members of her council, ladies in waiting, and yeomen of the guard assembled on the Tower green. She could see the Bell Tower with its three narrow Gothic windows, her former prison. She could not see the Traitor's Gate below the massive walls along the Thames. Bursts of music, choirs of children singing, and then the roar of cannon greeted her.

It was a cold winter's day but the snow stopped just in time and bright sunshine caught the glitter of jewels and gold. Elizabeth, in a royal robe of gold cloth and ermine cape, was carried in a gilded open litter. Gentlemen in crimson damask bearing gilt-edged battle-axes walked on either side. The silver and gold letters E R (Elizabeth Regina) on the footmen's velvet jerkins glistened in the sun. It was a long slow procession, stopping for pageants and musical demonstrations along the way. Gay banners fluttered from the windows, rich tapestries and embroidered velvets adorned the buildings. Occasionally the litter paused for Elizabeth to receive a gift. Smiling graciously, she accepted each offering with gratitude, whether a gold purse, an English Bible, or a little nosegay given by a farm girl. She knew how to please her people.

The following day she was anointed and crowned at the great Westminster Abbey. In crimson velvet and short ermine cape the stately queen walked over the purple carpet into the brilliantly lighted church. First she was crowned with the crown of state, then with the little crown of her brother, Edward, of pearls, diamonds, and sapphires. As she was presented to the people the sound of trumpets, fifes, and organ, of the church bells ringing overhead was "as if the world were coming to an end."

It was not easy to be a fascinating young woman and rule a kingdom. Many difficult things confronted her, above all an empty treasury and religious discontent. Elizabeth first showed her wisdom in choosing William Cecil as her chief adviser, for he was already schooled in the arts of governing and he was honest and wise, eager to spend hours of toil for the good of the country. With his help and that of the wizard financier, Thomas Gresham, Elizabeth gradually put England on a sound monetary system.

Economical herself, she was a help in cutting down expenses and building up a sound economy.

Elizabeth was not a deeply religious person. She belonged to the Renaissance, not the Reformation. Her interests lay in learning, art, music and dancing, the joys of the world. She had little sympathy for Puritans, the extreme Protestants, who wanted to reform everything; but she knew that to be English and Protestant were almost the same thing now. Her greatest interest was her subjects, and she did not want to offend either Catholics or Protestants, nor did she have any desire to pry into men's souls and consciences. She hoped for a workable religion which would satisfy most of her people. With the help of Parliament and her adviser, Cecil, she set about to establish a middle-of-the-road policy. The result was the Anglican Church of England, a national church which Elizabeth, like her father, Henry VIII, freed from ties with Rome and the Pope. Elizabeth re-established the use of English Bibles and prayer books which Mary had banned. She stopped religious persecution and substituted a mild punishment, a small fine, for not attending church. This made it easy for rich Catholics who did not want to attend the Anglican Church, and any Catholic could worship as he pleased in his own home.

Another problem Elizabeth had to face was marriage, or so everyone thought. How could a young woman alone manage a court which was mostly masculine, as well as rule a kingdom? Besides, she must produce an heir. But Elizabeth had probably decided long ago never to marry. Perhaps ghosts of the past troubled her: both her mother and her stepmother were married, then beheaded. Or maybe she did not want to share her role as monarch of the realm. Whatever the reason, Elizabeth played a good game, pretending interest now in one prince, now another. She kept her suitors dangling and hoping. It was good politics and it appeased her people. She once told Parliament, "I am already bound unto a husband which is the kingdom of England."

Elizabeth soon proved she could not only manage her court with ease but also make it the most brilliant court of the day. With her Renaissance education she could match the learning of any of her courtiers. She wrote poetry and songs and when she spoke her flow of words rose to golden eloquence. She knew how to stir men's souls. With her feminine coquetry, her skill in music and dancing, she won their admiration. Her court became tinged with romance and courtiers vied with each other in bursts of lyrical poetry or precious gifts to win the favor of the lady queen.

Elizabeth's skill in languages made her role as monarch easier. She could converse in Latin, Italian, French, and Spanish. She was as good in the game of diplomacy as any European ambassador. She rarely lost control of herself and her occasional bursts of temper were mild in comparison with the unbridled tempers of the men around her. She soon proved she could rule her country as well as, if not better than, a king.

Now that Elizabeth was queen she gave up her simple elegance and took to the most luxuriant Renaissance styles of the day, a mixture of Italian, French, and Spanish dress. Her dresses usually had wide, pleated ruffs which were tinged with gold or silver or adorned with jewels. The extreme pointed bodice of her gowns contrasted with the wide farthingale, a sort of hooped skirt, covered in rich brocades or velvet. Elizabeth adorned her hair with strings of pearls or diamonds. She wore high heels, as did all men and women of nobility to raise them above the dirt of the streets. Elizabeth, proud of her white skin, made it even whiter by using a lotion of egg whites, powdered eggshells, borax, and poppy seeds. She used delicate perfume made from marjoram. Her long slender fingers were covered with rings. Around her neck hung ropes of pearls or a gold collar, studded with jewels. She was once given a pair of silk knitted stockings which delighted her. "They are pleasant, fine and delicate," she said, and henceforth she wore them instead of the old cloth variety. This was a showy age and Elizabeth enjoyed being the most important show in all the land.

Dancing and music were important to Elizabeth, and to gain her favor a courtier must be accomplished in the latest dance steps, able to sing and play an instrument. Elizabeth herself could play the lute and the new keyboard instrument from Italy, the virginal.

She was also expert at the latest dance from Italy, *la volta,* which was described thus:

> Yet there is one, the most delightful kind,
> A lofty jumping or a leaping round.

It was much livelier than the waltz it later turned into.

Elizabeth, like other monarchs of the day, went on frequent progresses (short trips) within her realm. Her entire court and all its trappings moved from one palace to another. Elizabeth's progresses were not only to allow a palace to air out and sweeten while she was away but also to show herself to the people and to satisfy her desire to get to the countryside. She would either go to another palace of her own or visit a favorite courtier. In and around London she progressed by barge on the Thames. The royal barge was rather like a Venetian gondola, covered with gay canopies and festooned with flowers. Court musicians played and sang as the barge glided slowly on the river.

In the summer of 1575, Elizabeth visited her favorite courtier, the Earl of Leicester, at Kenilworth Castle. Twelve miles was the most the huge cavalcade of courtiers and carts of clothes and equipment could do in a day, for the roads were full of bumps and muddy ruts. There were many stops along the way to Kenilworth. Each village greeted the queen with pageants and gifts.

> Oh, blessed be the hour!
> Our Queen is coming to the Town
> With princely train and power.

ran a little song among the village folk preparing for her arrival.

Stopping at Oxford University, she patiently sat through a classical drama put on by the students and listened to Latin and Greek orations. Elizabeth enjoyed all types of plays and pageants, even the amateurish drama of students. Later in her reign Elizabeth's interest and support of the great dramatists such as Shakespeare kept the theater alive in spite of Puritan attempts to suppress it. Her appreciation of these efforts to entertain her, no matter how simple, gained her the love and admiration of all her people.

Elizabeth entering Kenilworth.

RADIO TIMES HULTON PICTURE LIBRARY, LONDON

Leicester, dressed in the lavish Renaissance style of the day, wore a tight-fitting brocaded doublet over which hung a short, jaunty velvet cape. Long hose came up to his short, puffed-out breeches. He bowed low, doffing his plumed cap as he greeted the queen and escorted her to the gates of the great palace.

Kenilworth, an old castle, had been transformed into a Renaissance palace by Henry VIII. Leicester had added to its magnificence. Set in the lovely rolling hills of Warwickshire, the palace was surrounded by a lake. Its newer buildings had spacious rooms and galleries with mullioned windows. Beautiful tapestries adorned the walls and a fifty-foot blue Turkish carpet ran the length of one room. Four-poster beds of carved wood had hangings of brilliantly colored velvets, edged in silver and gold. Glass lent its magic in large mirrors and glass candelabra. There was a chess table of silver and gold inlaid with precious stones. Outside lovely flower beds surrounded a large marble fountain whose cooling waters fell into a hexagonal pool.

As the queen paused on the bridge over the lake, a tiny island, sparkling with lights, floated toward her. A sea nymph chanted, "I am the lady of the lake. The lake, the lodge, the lord are yours for to command."

A salute of guns greeted the queen as she entered the courtyard. The large blue and gold clock on one of the towers was stopped, for time was to stand still while Elizabeth stayed at Kenilworth. As darkness set in, the castle on the green became a fairy palace, glittering with the light of candles and torches shining through the large glass windows. A display of fireworks was reflected in the pool. The entertainment was long but varied during the nineteen days Elizabeth stayed at Kenilworth. One day she went hunting, and when she returned a barge filled with musicians greeted her with sweet music. There was the more violent but popular entertainment of bearbaiting, in which a bear was set upon by dogs. Blood flowed freely and the people cheered as the savage beast lashed out and clawed at the snarling dogs which beset him from every angle. The bearbaiting was followed by Latin speeches and a classical play. For such was the curious mixture of Renaissance interest that men and women in those days could turn with equal enthusiasm from gross brutality to lofty speeches or lyrical poetry.

The last entertainment was a water pageant at twilight. Again the lady of the lake appeared on her floating island with twinkling lights and announced the Greek story to be enacted. A mechanical dolphin, concealing musicians in its belly, carried a youth whose sweet voice enticed a mermaid with an eighteen-foot tail! The audience was spellbound at these wondrous inventions. At the feast following in the large hall the table was laden with food. Three hundred different dishes were served: all kinds of meat, fowl and fish, sauces, breadstuffs, and sweets. French and Spanish wines sparkled in Venetian goblets. Elizabeth, however, ate little, as was her habit, and when she stopped eating everyone else did too. The servants who fed on leftovers did well that July at Kenilworth. The cost of all this entertainment was prodigious. Queen Elizabeth's visits were expensive honors.

But Elizabeth's reign was not all show and glitter. Her progresses were a sort of summer vacation from affairs of state, which she never neglected.

Elizabeth spent long hours of toil on governing her realm and

Sir Francis Drake.

FOLGER SHAKESPEARE LIBRARY, WASHINGTON

she expected her councilors to do the same. She had brought England out of chaos and bankruptcy to peace and prosperity. Her clever diplomacy kept her enemies divided, but peace was short-lived in those days and to keep the balance of power without war was a delicate business then, as indeed it is now.

Elizabeth's peace was an uneasy one, and England's need to expand trade caused rivalry with Spain. For many years England had sent its greatest product, wool, to the Netherlands, but the Netherlands, struggling for its independence, was on the brink of war with Spain. Spain began to block this trade to keep English goods from reaching the Netherlands.

England envied Spain's monopoly of the New World. She felt she had a right to explore and claim parts of the vast new continent not yet settled by Spain. But when England attempted to explore the New World or to trade with Spanish colonies trouble began.

In 1567, John Hawkins and Francis Drake, rugged adventurers, sailed to the West Indies with cargoes of woolen goods and slaves from Africa. In the dead of night, while their small boats lay at anchor, they were treacherously attacked by a large Spanish fleet. Drake and Hawkins fought their way free but many of their crew perished at the stake, burned by the Spanish Inquisitors, or were sold as slaves. Drake was so enraged that he swore to avenge this deed or die in the attempt. From then on he felt free to raid Spanish treasure ships and bring the prizes home to his queen. This clash with Spain was a first step leading to war—so far as

Drake was concerned, he was already at war with Spain. He became so successful at raiding the Spanish Main and looting Spanish treasure ships that he was known to Spaniards as the Terror of the Seas.

Elizabeth was secretly pleased with Drake's piracy. She could use the treasure. But to maintain the peace with Spain she had to frown on him officially. In 1577, against the advice of Cecil, Elizabeth supported a dangerous undertaking. She was taking a great risk for the glory and prestige of her country. She gave Drake money and backing for a voyage around the world. Officially he was to search for a continent south of South America. Secretly Elizabeth gave him permission to pick up what Spanish treasure he could. Everyone knows the story of this courageous voyage around the world, the second in history, the first by an Englishman. Having lost all but his own ship, the *Golden Hind,* in the stormy Straits of Magellan, Drake nevertheless captured a huge Spanish treasure ship off the Pacific coast of South America, explored the coast of California, and claimed it for the queen. In 1580, after nearly three years, Drake sailed proudly into Plymouth Harbor. His enormous treasure of millions of gold pieces was graciously received and Queen Elizabeth dined on board the *Golden Hind* and dubbed the courageous explorer and pirate Sir Francis Drake.

Drake's trip increased the prestige of England, but it brought England closer to a war with Spain. Other forces were at work which brought the threat even closer.

One of these forces was Elizabeth's cousin, Mary Queen of Scots, next in line to the English throne and a devout Catholic. A fugitive from Protestant Scotland, she had thrown herself on Elizabeth's mercy. But it was soon clear that Mary was involved in countless Catholic plots backed by Spain to overthrow Elizabeth and have herself established queen of England. She had to be closely watched, and Elizabeth had her made prisoner.

Elizabeth still hoped for peace but things seemed to be closing in and the threat of war was darkening the horizon. Spain was blockading English merchant ships in the Channel. English ships were pirating Spanish treasure. There was talk of a Spanish invasion and Spain was preparing a mighty armed fleet, the Armada.

Elizabeth's council realized that Mary was a source of trouble and conspiracy in England. How much she was a leader of plots, how much just the tool of plotters, it was hard to say, but it was clear that she was the center of treasonable ideas. The council urged Elizabeth to have her executed, but Elizabeth kept postponing the issue. She remembered her own unhappy time of confinement when she had been accused of plotting against her sister Mary. She could not bring herself to execute her kinswoman of royal blood.

But in 1586 a plot was uncovered which clearly revealed Mary's guilt in planning Elizabeth's murder and giving aid to the Spanish invasion of England. Elizabeth's clever councilor, Francis Walsingham, uncovered the plot by means of his intricate system of spies. He used an agent trusted by Mary but really working for him. The agent smuggled letters, in code, to and from Mary in beer kegs. They went in with the keg full of beer, inserted with the cork. They came out in the empty beer keg. Every time a letter went in or out the agent faithfully copied it and sent it straightway to Walsingham, who had it deciphered. When Walsingham had enough evidence plus the names of the conspirators, he divulged the plot.

This was treason and Elizabeth agreed to have Mary put to trial.

At Fotheringhay Palace the commissioners met and pronounced Mary guilty. Elizabeth hesitated to sign the death warrant. Ghosts of former queens haunted her. But in the end her long, delicate fingers drew the elaborate signature on the death warrant.

Mary, who had always had a sense of drama, staged the last act of her life well. She claimed to be a martyr for her religion. Dressed in black and holding a crucifix before her, she approached the execution block with dignity and calm. On the platform the captive queen turned and faced her audience. "I shall die as I have lived in the true and holy Catholic faith." The executioner removed her black robe, revealing a crimson gown beneath, the very color of martyrdom. She laid her head upon the block. Two strokes of the ax were heard. Her wig slipped from her head, revealing sparse gray hair. Her little dog crawled out from under her skirts but would not leave her corpse.

When news of Mary's death reached London the people went wild with joy. Their queen was safe—safe for the moment at least from foreign, Catholic plots. Bonfires were lit in the streets and church bells rang.

The moment of safety was brief, however, for Queen Elizabeth now knew that war with Spain was inevitable. Mary's death was the excuse Philip needed; he must avenge it, depose the heretic queen, and take the English throne himself.

Francis Drake was impatient to launch the war with Spain. He wanted to open the attack right away. Boatyards had been busy for a long time. The improvement in the navy started by Henry VIII had continued. All England's hopes lay in her navy, for she had no real standing army. Her new galleons (warships) were fast-sailing and armed in a new way, with rows of cannon for shooting long distances. The English ships were slimmer in proportion to their width than Spanish galleons. They were more streamlined and easier to maneuver. The high "castles" fore and aft, easy targets, had been lowered in English ships to give more space for mounting culverin, big long-range cannon which replaced less powerful and inaccurate stubby cannon.

Beheading of Mary Queen of Scots.

FOLGER SHAKESPEARE LIBRARY, WASHINGTON

The English idea was to avoid close contact with the enemy fleet and to destroy it by shooting "broadsides" from a distance. The Spanish, on the other hand, with fewer and less good cannon, still used medieval tactics. They counted on closing in with the enemy, boarding their ships, and fighting hand to hand.

John Hawkins was in charge of the shipbuilding and was rightly proud of the English navy, which could outsail and outgun any other. It was the newest and most powerful navy in all Europe. Hawkins, like Drake, was impatient to try it out.

Every port along the southern coast was equipped with a beacon to be lighted at the first sight of the Armada. This would be the alert to the country.

The Spanish plan for the invasion of England was to use both its Armada and land forces. The Spanish fleet was to sail north from Spain and join its army, then stationed in the Netherlands under the command of the Spanish general, the Duke of Parma. The Armada was to escort Parma's troops to the nearest landing point in England. But the Dutch, who had been secretly helped by the English, had control of all the seaports of the Netherlands coast line. Just how Parma could get his Spanish soldiers out to join the Armada was a problem which had not been solved.

Yet the odds were on a Spanish victory. Spain had had many victories and it seemed impossible that little England could withstand the might of the great Spanish Empire. Though the new English ships might be superior, the huge Spanish Armada with its well-trained soldiers was still thought to be invincible. To most of Europe it looked as though England were doomed.

In the spring of 1587, Elizabeth was worried and sad. The execution of Mary Queen of Scots hung heavily on her and now the war she had hoped to avoid seemed imminent. And she did not know where to turn for the money needed to keep her navy adequately manned. So she allowed Drake to go on another of his unofficial raids on the Spanish harbors.

Elizabeth now showed her art of clever, dissembling diplomacy. When she knew that Drake was well on his way to Spain, too far to be recalled, she publicly ordered him to return. To all Europe it appeared that Drake had gone of his own will and that Elizabeth was not instigating war. She was able to go on negotiating for peace.

Drake's raid on Cadiz Harbor, where many of the Spanish vessels lay at anchor, was far more successful than Elizabeth had dared to hope. Not only did Drake do irreparable damage to the Spanish fleet, burning and sinking thousands of tons of shipping and supplies, he also captured another huge treasure ship. No wonder the Spaniards thought him scarcely human. They even suspected he had a magic mirror which revealed to him just where the most important treasure ships lay.

Elizabeth was delighted at this setback for Spain, which would have to repair and replenish its fleet. It would delay the invasion of England. It gave England time to strengthen her fortifications and some money to equip a small land army.

It was not until July 19, 1588, that the first Spanish sails were sighted from the English shore. Slowly and majestically, the Invincible Armada loomed over the horizon. It was like a great seagoing crusade, red crosses on the sails, gay banners flying at the mastheads. Awesome and impressive, it moved in perfect precision, in a crescent shape, ever nearer to the tip of southwestern England. On shore the first of the beacons was lighted. Then one after another the beacons along the coast burst into flame. Soon even London knew that the dreaded Armada had come at last.

On first seeing the huge Armada, Englishmen's confidence was somewhat shaken. They thought they had never seen such a formidable array of fighting ships.

The Spanish commander of the fleet, Medina Sidonia, had a definite plan: to lure the English ships within the oval of his crescent, then close in its great crablike pincers. In this trap the English would be forced to fight a close battle, the Spanish would board the English ships and fight hand to hand. The Spanish knew they could count on their well-trained soldiers.

But as the Spanish viewed the English fleet from a distance their confidence, too, was somewhat shaken. The English ships, though large, seemed to have such speed. They darted this way and that with the greatest ease, able to tack and come about quickly. They

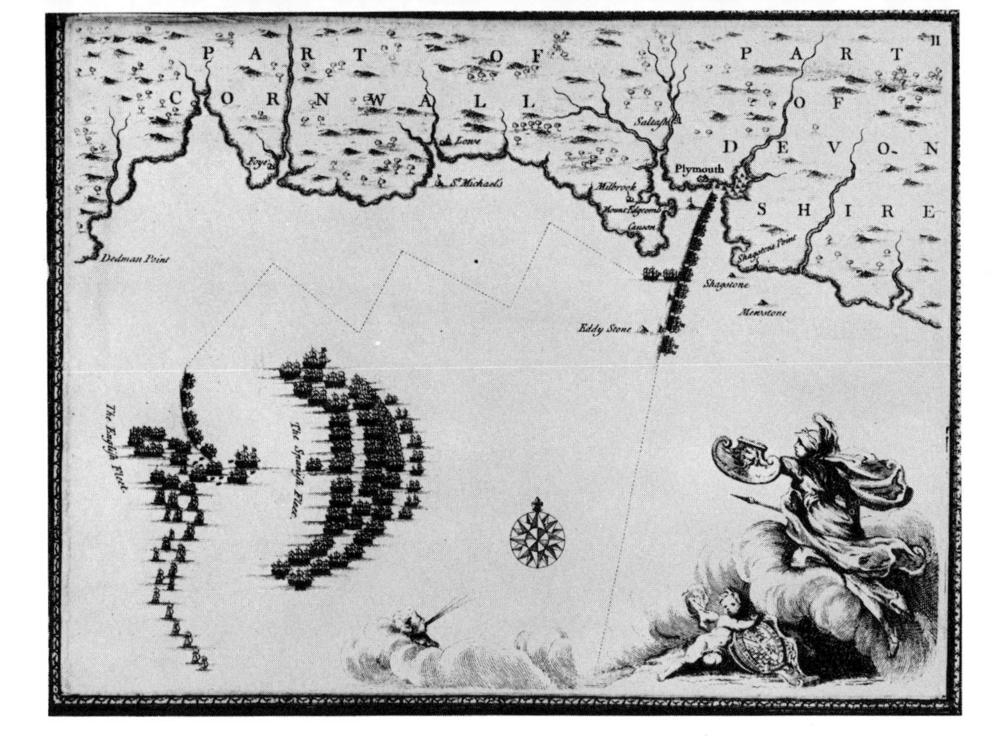

Armada in crescent formation in early state of battle in channel. The zigzag track shows how the English tacked out of Plymouth harbor and assembled to harass the Spanish.

had no formation and the Spanish could not tell how many there were. But they knew that Drake, Hawkins, and Frobisher, rugged men of the sea, were in those English ships.

The first few skirmishes did little damage to either fleet. The Spanish were annoyed, for they seemed unable to lure the English into their crescent trap. The English ships seemed fairly to dance in an insolent way. They would dart in, delivering cannon shot, and then speed away, out of reach. And yet they were not able to break up the great defensive formation of the Armada.

By July 27 both fleets were close to the narrowest part of the Channel, Calais Roads, where Medina Sidonia hoped to get in contact with Parma and his land forces. The English watched from a distance as the Spanish fleet dropped anchor. At only a long culverin-shot distance (about two miles) the English dropped anchor too. Here at least the English were close enough to their shore to be reinforced with ammunition and more ships.

Medina Sidonia did not know that Parma was helplessly trapped in the Netherlands. The Dutch were closely guarding all ports.

The English did not know it either; they were sure that Parma and his army were about to join the Armada. They must do something quickly.

The idea of fire ships seemed worth a try. Tide and wind would be right that night. Eight boats were chosen to be sacrificed and every combustible imaginable was put aboard them; the guns were loaded and the sails set.

At midnight the Spanish first noticed lights. There had been rumors that the English had invented hell burners, diabolical bomb boats which exploded. As they saw the flickering lights in the distance they were terror-stricken. Drake, they knew, was capable of anything.

Driving fast with the wind and current, straight toward the Armada, two by two came the fire ships. Spanish pinnaces were ordered to seize the fire boats with huge grapnels and tow them ashore before they did any damage. But this was not so easy, for the huge fire ships were coming at great speed, with wind and tide to help them. When the guns and cannon began to explode, sending random shots, panic seized the Spanish fleet, cables were cut and ships scattered; blown north and east by the increasing winds, the great crescent formation was broken at last.

The next morning the Spanish fleet had partially reassembled near the town of Gravelines on the Dutch coast. The English, reinforced and confident after the night's success, decided to get in closer to the enemy. Into the sides, onto the decks of the Spanish ships they sent shot after shot, gun shot and cannon balls. The Spanish soldiers, close-packed on the exposed decks, fought valiantly but hopelessly. Superior English guns were doing their damage. The decks of the Armada flowed with the blood of dead and wounded. As one boat heeled over, blood could be seen pouring from the scuppers. But late in the afternoon a sudden squall with blinding rain broke up the fighting.

The Spanish fleet was in dire distress with many crippled ships and little ammunition. The food situation was alarming. Faulty barrels made of green wood had turned water to a green slime and food rancid. The damage Drake had done to Spanish shipping and stores in his raid on Cadiz was telling now. The wind was blowing hard and the galleons were dangerously near the shallows.

But again the wind shifted and with gale-like force began to blow the Spanish north and west, between Norway and Scotland. The English pursued as far as the Firth of Forth. Even then the gallant Armada tried to reassemble into its crescent, expecting to fight the battle to its bitter end. But there was no choice. With the unwieldy ships, many of which were sinking fast, they had to go north with the wind, and then with luck west around the tip of Scotland, and south past Ireland to home waters in Spain. Many of the damaged ships were wrecked on the coasts of Scotland and Ireland. Survivors, seeking refuge on shore, were savagely slaughtered. Of the one hundred and thirty ships which had left Spain less than half returned. Only one third of the fighting men returned, most of them sick or wounded.

While the English pursued the Spanish up the North Sea, Queen Elizabeth set out by barge from London to Tilbury where her land troops were assembled. Wild rumors spread the fear that Parma and his army were on their way and about to land. The English as yet had no news of the rout of the Spanish fleet. In spite of fears for Elizabeth's safety, she insisted on visiting her troops. Now that this war that she had so hoped to avoid had come, Elizabeth's courage was an inspiration. Dressed in white velvet and mounted on a white horse, she rode among her troops. She consented to wear a silver cuirass but was bareheaded, her plumed helmet carried by a page. Coming to her army like this, with the enemy possibly only a few hours away, the queen made a great impression. She dismounted and walked among her soldiers, giving them courage in the hour of danger. She said she had come to live and die amongst them in the heat of battle, and she added these stirring words: "I know I have the body of a weak and feeble woman but I have the heart and stomach of a king, and of a king of England, too, and think foul scorn that Parma or Spain or any prince in Europe should dare to invade the borders of my realm." The soldiers went wild with enthusiasm. There was no question but that they would die for their beloved, fearless queen.

When news of the victory was received the nation rejoiced and praised God. The saying was, "God blew and the enemy dispersed." That the little island state had triumphed over the powerful Spanish Empire seemed a miracle. Now England would be free to use the seas, to explore new lands, to trade, and even to plant new colonies.

Elizabeth with English and Spanish galleons in background.

RADIO TIMES HULTON PICTURE LIBRARY, LONDON

The defeat of the Spanish Armada did not end the war with Spain but from then on the prestige of the great Catholic empire began to wane. And the prestige of England began to rise. The feeling of patriotism and national pride was at its peak. Even the English Catholics remained loyal to their queen, and when the news of the victory reached Rome, young English students at a Catholic college burst into cheers. To be an Englishman seemed more important than one's religion. And the symbol of England's unity and glory was the queen, now also queen of the sea. She was the very spirit of this new and glorious England.

Even her enemy the Pope paid her a compliment. "She is certainly a great queen. Just look how she governs! She is only a woman, only mistress of half an island, and yet she makes herself feared by Spain, by France, by the Empire, by all."

In November 1588 the victory was celebrated by a procession to St. Paul's Cathedral. London was decked out as gaily as it had been for the coronation day. Spanish banners, captured in the battle, hung from the gate on London Bridge, a gayer sight than the usual heads of criminals. The queen rode in one of the new open coaches instead of a litter. Elizabeth, "all in white, sitting alone in her splendid coach, looked like a goddess." Ballads, songs, and music filled the air with praises of the queen and her glorious triumph over Spain.

Elizabeth was fifty-four in the year of the Armada. Her face looked older, she relied more heavily on cosmetics, and she had taken to wearing a wig. But her body and her spirit were as young as ever. She still enjoyed exercise, walking, riding fast, and dancing. Every morning she danced several galliards to keep herself in good condition. Her slim, graceful figure looked no more than that of a young girl of sixteen. She often dressed in white velvet or taffeta trimmed with silver, possibly to live up to her goddesslike role.

She still loved flattery and her courtiers praised her to the skies. Competition to do their best for the queen sharpened their wits. A burst of song and poetry, praising the queen and England, brought forth the greatest artistic achievement of her reign, Elizabethan literature. The English language reached its peak of beauty and men and women delighted in the use and sound of words. Lyrics, love sonnets, and ballads issued from the court and swept the country in a wave of verbal intoxication. A young man, William Shakespeare, began writing in poetic and immortal words of the deeds and the heroism of England's past.

It was a new era of confidence and patriotism. Young men were eager to go off to war against their enemy, Spain, and to subdue their rebellious neighbor, Ireland, or to set out across the seas for wealth and conquest, to plant new colonies in the name of the queen. Elizabeth shared their enthusiasm. She too wanted wealth and new trade for her country and above all glory for her reign.

Even before the battle of the Armada, men other than Drake and Hawkins had sailed the cold north seas near Canada, searching for a northwest passage. A few years before the battle Sir Humphrey Gilbert had explored and claimed Newfoundland for the queen. His attempt to plant a colony there had failed and he had died in a shipwreck. But his young stepbrother, Sir Walter Raleigh, was inspired by the same hope of planting a colony in America.

Walter Raleigh was one of Elizabeth's favorite courtiers, an accomplished young Renaissance man. Handsome and brilliant, a poet and a dandy, he also had the reckless daring of that age. Captain of the Queen's Guard, he soon grew rich on royal favors. He dressed lavishly; even his shoes sparkled with jewels and he was looked upon with envy by other courtiers. As a youth he had lived among seafaring men on the southern coast of England. In spite of the attractions of court life, his greatest passion, in his own words, was "to seek new worlds for gold, for praise, for glory." He dreamed of starting a new nation in the New World, a new England. But during the 1580s, Elizabeth could not spare him from court and he had to content himself with financing and sending expeditions to the land he hoped to settle. His first expedition in 1584 reconnoitered the coast north of Florida and brought back such glowing accounts of rich land and friendly natives that Raleigh named the territory Virginia, in honor of his virgin queen. In 1585, Raleigh sent one hundred settlers to plant a colony on Roanoke Island. Running short of provisions, they stayed there only a year. A third expedition was sent in 1587 with men and women and high hopes of a permanent colony. This was the famous "lost colony" which vanished without a trace. Probably the settlers perished at the hands of the Indians. It was not easy to establish colonies three thousands miles away, in an unknown wilderness, but Raleigh did not give up hope. In fact it was the vision and perseverance of such men as Raleigh that paved the way to England's future colonization all over the world. Even though Raleigh's prime motive was gold and glory, he had made a first step toward the settlement of North America. And even from prison where he later spent many years he wrote of Virginia, "I shall yet live to see it an English nation."

Raleigh and his companions did not find gold in the New World. They did find two products which put Virginia on the map: potatoes and tobacco. These Raleigh helped to popularize and they soon were worth their weight in gold. Potatoes were a rare delicacy and tobacco was considered to have medicinal properties.

Elizabeth supported these overseas ventures, often against the advice of her council and often with her own money. She too helped sow the seeds of colonization in America. Her struggle with Spain to obtain freedom of the seas and an open door to settlement in America finally was successful in the reign of the next monarch, James I. But Elizabeth lived to launch the great East India Trading Company in 1599, which brought wealth and fame and was the beginning of the British Empire.

The new prosperity was felt everywhere, in people's lavish dress, the luxury of the new buildings, the leisure to study, to write or compose music. Young men flooded the universities of Oxford and Cambridge and the law schools in London. Many went abroad to study, to Italy and France, bringing back foreign styles and refined Renaissance manners. Music was everywhere, not only at court but even in barbershops, which provided musical instruments for young men waiting to have their beards trimmed. Music even accompanied explorers. Drake took his company of musicians around the world.

Wealthy nobles built mansions of stone or brick with Italian marble decorations. These buildings were often in the shape of an E, in honor of the queen. There was a rage for glass; more and bigger windows were put in houses. "Hardwick Hall, more glass than wall" described a new Renaissance palace of three stories with huge glass windows. There was a rage for chimneys too, chimneys not for use but just for decoration with intricate brickwork designs.

The Earl of Essex.

NATIONAL PORTRAIT GALLERY, LONDON

Beautiful formal gardens were laid out with care. The English had always loved flowers, and new varieties, shrubs and hedges and fruit trees were brought in from Italy. Elizabeth's lovely Greenwich Palace on the Thames has unfortunately disappeared. Of pink-red brick, it was surrounded by gardens and green lawns sloping toward the river. Its tilting green was the scene of tournaments and pageants.

The brilliance of Elizabeth's court was sometimes marred by the violence of rivals seeking her favor. Tempers grew hot and duels were frequent. Intrigues got out of hand and even threatened the safety of the queen. When a new young favorite, the Earl of Essex, began to take the place of Raleigh, rival groups split the court in two.

Essex, young, handsome, and romantic, had irresistible charms. His courage and daring and his skill at jousting made him a popular hero too.

Essex's rise in Elizabeth's affections and to fame and glory was fast—too fast, in fact. It went to his head. Once, in a huff, he dared to turn his back on the queen, an unheard-of breach of etiquette. Furious, for the queen would take no insubordination even from a favorite, Elizabeth flew at him and boxed his ears, ordering him to be gone from the court.

But the queen had a weakness for this fiery young man. He was soon back at court, more prominent and arrogant than ever. Seeking more fame and power, Essex asked to go to Ireland to suppress the rebels there. But his expedition was a complete failure. He acted in a highhanded way, openly disobeyed the queen's orders, and wasted money and men.

Elizabeth's fury was white-hot. Essex, knowing her anger and fearing his enemies at court, decided to vindicate himself. Counting on the queen's affection for him, he deserted his post and dashed to London. Bursting in upon the queen, unannounced and splattered with mud and dirt, he covered her hands with kisses. But Elizabeth was not to be put off by his charms this time. She had him arrested and put in custody.

It was difficult to keep this hotheaded Essex in confinement. He was still popular in spite of his behavior. Soon he was released but still barred from court and honors. Away from court he brooded. In his wounded pride he harbored resentment, and dark ambition kindled in his breast. Ambition turned to thoughts of treason. He convinced himself and his friends that his enemies were after his life, that the only thing to do was to take London, storm the court, and force the queen at sword's point to restore him to power and wealth.

Shouting, "A plot is laid for my life," Essex and his followers started for the city. But again failure stalked this ambitious man. The popular hero counted on London rising to his defense. Instead he was greeted by alarmed silence. No one ventured to take up arms in his cause. And when the word "traitor" was heard, the crowds, even some of his friends, began to slink away. Aghast and desperate, the once proud Essex realized there was nothing to do but surrender.

A week later Essex and five of his fellow conspirators were condemned to death for treason. Dramatic to the end as Mary Queen

Queen Elizabeth in Parliament.

FOLGER SHAKESPEARE LIBRARY, WASHINGTON

of Scots had been, Essex appeared before the execution block all in black. As he flung his cloak aside he showed a scarlet waistcoat. He met his death bravely and humbly asked forgiveness for this "vilest traitor who has ever lived." Men and women of those days knew how to die, sometimes with a touch of drama or a jest but always with courage.

Elizabeth knew that the welfare of her state and the safety of the crown demanded Essex's head, but she could not shake her grief over his death. His popularity lingered long in the minds of the people. "Sweet England's pride is gone." Some of the joy of Elizabeth's reign seemed to go with the death of Essex. Other heroes were going too. Drake and Hawkins died on a last voyage to the West Indies, and then her wise old statesman, Cecil.

In 1601, Elizabeth called her Parliament. Though she had the imperious, iron hand of her father she ruled more wisely. She knew it was important to work with Parliament, if possible, and not against it.

At this, her last parliament, Elizabeth listened to complaints. Members objected to the queen's rewarding her favorites by allowing them to tax things like salt and wine. This made the rich richer and the poor poorer. Elizabeth agreed to remove these unfair "monopolies." When members of Parliament, with joy and deep-felt gratitude, came to thank the queen, Elizabeth addressed them in these golden words:

"Though God hath raised me high, yet this I account the glory of my crown, that I have reigned with your loves. . . . And though you have had and may have mightier and wiser princes sitting in this seat, yet you never have had nor shall have any that will love you better."

Elizabeth's spirit and energy lasted until her death. At the age of sixty-seven, when some of her courtiers grumbled at the idea of a long progress, Elizabeth bade the old stay behind and the young and able go with her.

The winter of 1603 was cold and damp and in January the court moved to Richmond, the warmest of her palaces. Elizabeth had enjoyed the Christmas revels and had even danced the coranto. But in March she caught a fever. She refused medicine and she refused to eat, sitting silent and pensive. Her coronation ring, which she had worn for forty-four years, had grown into her flesh and had to be sawed off. Perhaps she felt this was the end of her "marriage" to her realm. She was ready to die, but sitting propped on cushions, she refused to lie down. Only when she fainted from weakness did they carry her to her bed.

As she lay dying it was said a strange silence descended on the city of London. No bells rang, no bugles sounded. On March 24 the glorious reign of England's greatest monarch and the last of the great Renaissance rulers came to an end.

The scholar Camden expressed the feelings of the English people when he said, "She was a queen who hath so long and with so great wisdom governed her kingdoms, as the like hath not been read or heard of, either in our own time or since the days of the Roman Emperor Augustus."

WILLIAM SHAKESPEARE

William Shakespeare.

FROM THE FIRST FOLIO EDITION OF HIS PLAYS

ONE day in late April of 1564, when Queen Elizabeth had been on the throne of England for only six years, a child was taken to be baptized in the small English country town of Stratford-on-Avon. The baby was the son of John Shakespeare, an important member of the town council and a maker of fine gloves. John and his wife, Mary, carried their newborn boy through streets lined by blossoming apple and pear trees to the old stone church close by the river; the blossoms and the gray church tower were reflected in the flowing waters of the Avon. The infant's name was entered on the parish register in neat handwriting and careful Latin: Gulielmus filius Johannes Shakspere (William, son of John Shakspere). The vicar, like every other educated person in England, spelled Latin accurately, but English as he pleased—and "Shakspere" was the spelling he chose to put down for the child's last name. William himself never made up his mind how to spell it. In the year of his death, 1616, he spelled it two different ways on the pages of his will.

These two documents—the baptismal record and the will—are among the few surviving records of Shakespeare's life, even though he is now celebrated as the greatest poet and playwright the world has ever known. Most of his life story is a mystery that has fascinated thousands of people who love his poems and plays and wish they knew more about him.

In those days dramatists were not considered important. Their plays were written quickly, for deadlines, and the manuscripts were often thrown away. No one bothered to preserve Shakespeare's manuscripts or letters. Nobody described his boyhood, his schooling, or his family.

We can guess from the faded paint on a statue made after his death that he was redheaded, and from a rather awkward engraving that he lost some of this red hair as a relatively young man; that his forehead was unusually high; that he grew a mustache and later a pointed beard; and that his expression was pleasant.

Fortunately a great deal is known about the Stratford of his boyhood and the exciting life that London offered young playwrights of Shakespeare's generation.

When William Shakespeare was born, Stratford-on-Avon was a thriving market town of about two thousand people. The river flowed along one side; a stone arched bridge was the town's only link with the main road to the university town of Oxford and to London, a metropolis of two hundred thousand people. Stratford's houses were of timber, plaster, and brick, and there were two fine inns, the Bear and the Swan, to attract the traveler. The Shakespeare family's big house with its massive chimney stack and strong timber roof was at one end of town. Near it was the place where stalls were put up for weekly market days and where John Shakespeare could display his supple, finely worked gloves. A few blocks beyond was the Grammar School, and beyond that, at the other end of town, the Holy Trinity Church where Shakespeare was baptized that April day. Gardens and tall trees abounded in the lovely town, and all around stretched fertile fields. Nearby was the Forest of Arden, full of deer and hare, and in the other direction the Cotswold hills rolled gently.

A splendid house called Charlecote was a few miles away, and here Queen Elizabeth stayed overnight on one of her summer progresses—when Shakespeare was two and a half. On her way back to London she did not turn left over the stone bridge to Stratford, but all the townspeople must have crossed the river and lined the banks to watch her go by in all her splendor. Perhaps Bailiff John Shakespeare, with his little boy Will at his side, made her a short speech of welcome and presented her with a gift.

Many of Will's boyhood hours were spent watching the animals and flowers of the nearby fields and woods. At other times he had to be in school. The Grammar School was free to the sons of town officials—and Shakespeare's father was the highest official in the town. The School days were long, from six in the summers and seven in the winters until five at night. Students were taught Bible, grammar, rhetoric, and writings of the ancient authors. Years later Shakespeare described

> . . . the whining schoolboy, with his satchel
> And shining morning face, creeping like snail
> Unwillingly to school.

A schoolroom in Shakespeare's day.

FOLGER SHAKESPEARE LIBRARY, WASHINGTON

He also wrote about "the threatening twigs of birch"—the usual punishment for inattentive children.

He was probably not very fond of school. Yet he learned his Latin and Bible well, and found time away from school to read everything he could lay his hands on. The Renaissance brought to England translations of the Greek classics and the latest French, Italian, and Spanish stories. Poems and songs and histories by Englishmen were being printed in profusion for the first time. A bright, inquiring boy like Will would naturally wheedle such books from anyone in Stratford who happened to own one.

Every summer Stratford was visited by strolling players, usually under the sponsorship of some nobleman. Dressed in their showiest costumes and preceded by a banging of drums and a trick dog or tumbling clown, these actors would walk into town. Some carried all their possessions in sacks on their backs. Other more fortunate players had wagons laden with curtains, ropes, clothes, pots and pans for cooking on the way, and a few simple props like crowns, wings, or lifelike decapitated heads for a beheading scene. First the actors had to get a license from Bailiff John Shakespeare. If he approved of their act, they were allowed to set up their stage in the middle of the market square. Sometimes they simply pushed their flat wagons together and used them for a stage; other times they put planks across barrels or trestles. A tent on one side of the stage was all they had in which to hide props or change costumes. All around swarmed the fascinated villagers, their heads barely stage-high, their smallest children on their shoulders, all gawking at the gaudy costumes, the fake moneybags and silver-painted swords of the actors. Then the play began, a performance of jigs and tricks and songs, with a simple skit or two in between. From 1573 to 1587 there are records of twenty-three such companies coming to Stratford.

Another sort of entertainment was put on every year at Coventry, only a twenty-mile horseback ride away. There the local guilds gave traditional religious plays dating back into the Middle Ages. Many well-loved episodes from the Bible were presented on curtainless platforms or pageant wagons surrounded on all sides by

Traveling players in a village square.

FROM PETER BREUGHEL THE YOUNGER, *A Village Fete*

the audience. Young Will probably saw Joshua commanding the sun to stand still, or the three wise men following the Star of the East, or, best of all, King Herod storming up and down in a rage. In one of these old plays which survives today, one can get a good idea of the English spoken by the Herod of four hundred years ago: "I rent! I raw! and now run I wode!" With these fine words Herod in his colorful robes indeed would run—right off the stage, jumping down among the spectators. Sometimes, if Herod were supposed to pursue the Holy Family, he would leap on his horse tethered to the stage and race through the streets of Coventry, frightening all the children.

Plays in local churches were another old form of entertainment. By means of a mechanism in the church roof beams, the actor Jesus and assorted saints could ascend to heaven. Even though the block and tackle that carried them there creaked and groaned in an obvious manner, the audience—particularly children—must have been very impressed.

These shows, with their acrobatic stunts and simple jokes and creaky stage effects, would not seem very good today. But they were all there were for a little country boy to see in England of the 1570s. Even the queen could not get much more sophisticated entertainment at the beginning of her reign. She had to hire the same companies of players that traveled through Stratford and other villages, with the same old short plays and stunts. But she could afford to have elaborate pageants added to their regular performances.

Eleven-year-old Shakespeare may have seen the fabulous water pageant with fireworks, a mechanical dolphin, and an actor dressed as a mermaid, which the Earl of Leicester presented for the queen at his great estate of Kenilworth, not far away from Stratford. Twenty years later Shakespeare wrote these lines in *A Midsummer Night's Dream:*

> . . . once I sat upon a promontory
> And heard a mermaid, on a dolphin's back . . .
> And certain stars shot madly from their spheres
> To hear the sea-maid's music.

Perhaps he was remembering the earl's fireworks and mechanical dolphin.

When Will was twelve his father had a change of fortune. For some mysterious reason, which no one has ever discovered, he retired from the town government and gradually lost most of his property. He failed to get a coat of arms for which he had hopefully applied. If he had ever planned to send his brightest son to a university, he could no longer afford to do so. Will's prospects were gloomy.

Other, luckier young men were able to go to the great universities at Oxford and Cambridge. Some of these students began to experiment with writing plays. These were presented in the huge torchlit university halls while musicians played, and the audience of enthusiastic students, ladies in huge farthingales, and courtiers in wonderful finery mingled on the crowded floor. Queen Elizabeth herself often came to watch the students' plays. Their plots were mainly copied from old Roman plays rediscovered by Renaissance scholars, and their language was often pompous and stiff-sounding, but they were the small beginnings of the great Elizabethan drama soon to come.

Shakespeare was not to see these plays or meet these young playwrights for many more years. He had to be content with life in a small town. He read hungrily of far lands and romantic places. Everyone was talking of Sir Francis Drake looting treasure ships off the Spanish Main, or of Sir Humphrey Gilbert landing on the coast of Newfoundland. England's world was expanding, but twelve-year-old Will Shakespeare's world was narrowing. The few glimpses he got of the great, expanding Elizabethan world were probably brought by the traveling players that walked the dusty roads to Stratford every summer.

These actors must have told him of their successes in the thriving city of London, where they set up temporary stages in the courtyards of the big inns like the Cross Keys and the Bell, and drew huge crowds. Higher-paying spectators would sit in the inns' balconies, looking down at the performance while the innkeepers served them with food and beer. The lesser folk as usual stood closely around the stage. But there was a serious problem for the actors when they rented a London inn-yard: the Puritans or the city-magistrates might forbid their performances at any time. The Puritans called the actors "masters of vice" and their plays the "inventions of the devil." The magistrates feared that the crowded, noisy gatherings might breed riot or plague. In 1576, an actor found a solution for these difficulties. He built a most unusual building north of the city walls, away from the criticisms of the Puritans and the jurisdiction of the lord mayor. But the most interesting thing about this building was that it was designed especially for the giving of plays. It was called—"The Theater"—for there were no others. At last life could be easier for actors, with a permanent stage and a permanent place behind the stage where they could change their costumes. It was open to the sky like a stadium, for daylight was the cheapest light available. The row or two of balconies for the richer classes were copied from the inns.

Plays were often performed in innyards like this.

FOLGER SHAKESPEARE LIBRARY, WASHINGTON

Money poured in from throngs of curious Londoners. The only drawback was the plays—still mostly jigs and dances, stiff speeches and slapstick jokes. Where was a writer to be found who could provide more inspiring fare for these crowds who were hungry for exciting plots, glorious spectacles, and fine words?

The person who later was going to provide all these things and more was at the moment a Stratford boy in his teens, going to school, working, reading voraciously and exploring the countryside.

Then, when only eighteen, Will Shakespeare married Anne Hathaway, the daughter of a prominent and respected man in a neighboring village across the meadows. She lived in a big black and white timbered house, and though today tourists call it "Anne Hathaway's cottage," it is very sizeable, with good paneling and well-carved furniture.

We do not know what Anne looked like or what kind of a person she was. But she was eight years older than Will. Early domesticity in a small town did not hold the young husband for long. At some point—we don't know when or how—he left Stratford to make his way in the world.

No records have yet been found of William Shakespeare's life from 1585, when his twins were born, until 1592 when London was buzzing with his name. Scholars have called this period "the seven lost years" and have filled many books trying to prove that he joined the army, or the navy, or became a lawyer, or went abroad with a rich lord. But it seems probable that he followed some traveling players back to London. In the summer of 1587, five companies of players came to Stratford. One might have been irresistible to Shakespeare, now twenty-three years old. When it left town noisily with trumpet and somersaulting clown, he might have left his wife and three children and followed it down the dusty road.

In any case, at some point he must have gone to work for a London theatrical company. Maybe he worked for several companies in succession, starting at the bottom with an unimportant job and gradually working up to small actors' parts. There is an old legend that he first held horses at one of the London theater doors. This tale may very well have some truth in it. He had to start somehow on his theatrical career and perhaps that is the first job he could get.

London in the 1580s provided a wonderful atmosphere for a young man who loved the stage and had a gift for heart-stirring language. The times were exciting. In the first part of the decade there was the real fear that the Spaniards would land their famous armies on English soil. By the end of the decade the Armada had been scattered, the Spanish power was broken, and Englishmen were exultant. Now the country was free to celebrate its triumph in music, poetry, and a new kind of drama. The old plays that had been so popular for hundreds of years would not do any more. They did not express what England was feeling.

There were now three London theaters—The Theater, The Curtain, and the Rose—and several other London companies who put on plays wherever they could. Among them they produced at least fifty plays a year. They were desperate for new material and there was not much of it. London audiences demanded excitement. If a play bored them, they could find plenty of entertainment elsewhere. They could go to the Bear Gardens and cheer appreciatively at the sight of a blind bear tied to a stake, mangling and crushing the dogs let loose on him. They could attend the frequent public hangings and watch the hangman quarter his victims while they were still alive. So any plays to draw audiences away from this sort of thing had to have gory action, with royal splendor and stirring words thrown in as an added attraction.

The first playwrights to meet this challenge were the university men, who moved into London to write new plays for the demanding London public. Two Oxford men, Lyly and Peele, and two Cambridge men, Greene and Nashe, had early successes. Another man, Kyd, wrote a melodrama called *The Spanish Tragedy* which did so well that it frightened and thrilled English audiences for twenty years. But the best and most successful of them all was Christopher Marlowe. Just Shakespeare's age, he came to fame earlier, for he started younger. All these men were writing successfully in the eighties—the years when William Shakespeare was just beginning to learn his craft. Their plays were full of Greek mythology and speeches in the lofty style of the ancient Romans; most of their plots were modeled on popular stories from Renaissance Italy. All had long, loud, rhythmical speeches, and as many violent characters and situations as possible: ghosts, madmen, murderers, and duels, beatings, and battles. But they also had moments of pure poetry and great beauty. The great age of Elizabethan drama was on its way.

The newcomer, Shakespeare, was impressed and inspired by these plays and by the men who wrote them. Acting soon was not enough for him—he began to try his hand at writing, too.

Writers often gathered in taverns like the famous *Mermaid,* to scribble last-minute lines, help each other with suggestions, sometimes all to share in scenes for a single play. Shakespeare gradually became a welcome member of these gatherings. At first he learned to write plays by copying others' tricks and styles. He patched up poor plays, wrote a few scenes here and there for others, and thus learned his trade as he went along. His employers must have felt lucky that their new actor could write and rewrite so easily, for without good plays they would lose their audiences and their livelihood.

The first play known as Shakespeare's own—a play based on English history of some one hundred and fifty years past—was *Henry VI.* It was full of everything the Elizabethan audiences loved: high-sounding words, noble personages in gorgeous costumes, surprise attacks, funerals, riots, duels, sorcery, and deaths. Bodies were carried off stage in scene after scene. A duke threatened to stamp upon a cardinal's hat and tug his beard. The French Joan of Arc summoned up fiends and spirits, dueled with an English duke, and was finally led off by the English to the stake. A lord shouted:

> "Frenchmen—
> Your hearts I'll stamp out with my horse's heels
> And make a quagmire of your mingled brains!"

And there was a particularly touching scene, which made the emotional audience sob loudly, in which the great English hero, Lord Talbot, died on the battlefield as his son lay dead in his arms.

This play, put on at the Rose Theater in March 1592 by Lord Strange's men, greatly pleased the spectators. It broke all records for attendance and made a huge profit for the company. The thousands who saw the play felt a great pride in their own splendid past. They had seen many plays based on biblical or classical stories, full of Herods and Caesars, but this was something new. These kings and queens and princes strutting about on stage were of a time not too far in the past and their glorious deeds were familiar to the oldest and youngest in the audience.

So popular was this play that Shakespeare quickly wrote three more in the same series—*Henry VI*, Parts 2 and 3; and *Richard III*. All had wicked characters conniving for the English throne, but Richard was the most wicked of all, gloating over his misdeeds and murdering his two little nephews in the Tower. The audience loved the great scene in which the ghost of one of the murdered princes came to visit the tent of Richard the night before the fatal battle of Bosworth Field, and groaned:

> "Think how thou stabst me in my prime of youth,
> Think on the Tower, and despair and die!"

And later, when Richard staggered on the battlefield and cried, "A horse! A horse! My kingdom for a horse!" the audience roared with glee and went home quoting the phrase over and over.

Shakespeare then tried his hand at a fashionable and rather typical classical tragedy. It was called *Titus Andronicus*. The plot called for several bloody heads to be brought on stage, and even for an actor to have his hand chopped off in full view. This was hard to manage realistically, when all the audience was so near to the stage. One actor had to bring his cleaver down quickly while at the same moment the other tucked back his hand into his sleeve and calf's blood spurted profusely! It must be added that the play ends with a mother eating her own sons in a pie—and also that it was a wild success.

While Shakespeare was grinding out these melodramas for the varied audience at the Rose or Curtain, he also experimented with comedies, and for these he had a special part of the audience in mind. This was an elegant group of young noblemen who loved to mingle with artists, leaving their splendid houses to join the noisy crowds thronging to the theaters. In their special sections of the balcony noblemen smoked tobacco and showed off their finery and spoke rudely, interrupting with hisses or loud applause. If an actor pleased them, they would entertain him in their own houses. If a play pleased them, they would ask the company to pack up and present it over again at palace or court. Shakespeare's company had to be ready at any moment for such an imperious summons.

Shakespeare observed these rich young men of the court, both at the theaters and at their own splendid establishments. He watched their sports and swordplay, heard their music, and studied their manners. Theirs were the "courtier's, soldier's, scholar's eye, tongue, sword; the glass of fashion and the mould of form"—typical Renaissance men like Lorenzo de' Medici of a century before. From them he got his final education. Because of his capacity to absorb impressions with lightning speed, it was easy for this country boy, now a leading dramatist, to learn their sophisticated tastes. He began to write comedies that he knew they would like: *Love's Labour's Lost, The Two Gentlemen of Verona,* and *The Comedy of Errors.* He borrowed parts of his plots from popular Italian stories, filled them with foreign-named characters, and set them in the Mediterranean cities that the rich young lords knew from their travels. But though he might be writing of life in Padua or Athens, English names like Bridget or Nell or Dobbin were likely to appear, and the Stratford countryside that Shakespeare loved so well kept cropping out. His most courtly play of those years ended with this song:

> When icicles hang by the wall,
> And Dick the shepherd blows his nail[1]
> And Tom bears logs into the hall
> And milk comes frozen home in pail,
> When blood is nipped and ways be foul,
> Then nightly sings the staring owl,
> "Tu-whit,
> To-who," a merry note,
> While greasy Joan doth keel[2] the pot.

In 1593 the Bubonic plague swept through London. As it spread a thousand people a week died. The churchbells rang without cease as victim after victim was carted to his grave. Puritans thundered that the cause of the plague was sin—and the cause of sin was the plays. All public gatherings were forbidden. The theaters of London were closed. Actors, producers and playwrights were thrown out of work for two desperate years.

But Shakespeare was lucky. Not only did he have many influential friends, but now he had a patron—the wealthy and handsome Earl of Southampton, then twenty years old. Shakespeare had hopefully sent a poem of some two hundred verses called *Venus and Adonis* to this rich young man, writing, "I know not how I shall offend in dedicating my unpolisht lines to your Lordship." The lines of course were not unpolished at all; the story told in them had a popular mythological plot and much suspense, and the earl had been delighted. The poem was rushed to the printer. All the earl's elegant friends demanded copies and it became a best seller. Soon Shakespeare dashed off another long poem, with a warmer dedication, showing that his friendship with his patron had grown close. This too was published, and sold well. Now Shakespeare the poet was considered a real writer, for all fashionable Elizabethans admired poetry but still considered drama rather vulgar, written merely to please the multitudes.

[1] Blows on his hands to warm them.
[2] Cool.

A young aristocrat of Shakespeare's day.

VICTORIA AND ALBERT MUSEUM, LONDON

So Shakespeare, with the help of his powerful patron, did not have to starve in a plague-ridden city. During the two years of the plague it is quite likely that he lived part of the time in one of the houses of the Earl of Southampton, outside of the city. Perhaps he spent much of this time with his family back in Stratford, its peaceful life now a relief from crowded, frightened London. He worked on new plays and started to write the long series of sonnets which are so beautiful that they alone would have put him at the head of all English poets. Legend says that the earl, delighted with his brilliant protégé, gave him a thousand pounds. It probably was nearer a hundred, for even this would be a handsome sum for those days—much more than the price of the large house which Shakespeare was soon to buy in Stratford.

Meanwhile the acting companies of London were having a bad time. Some had to pawn the expensive costumes they had collected through the years, others took to the road and never came back to the city again. But some of the best actors and managers managed to scrape through and form new companies when the plague was over.

When the Lord Chamberlain's Company was organized in 1594, Shakespeare not only joined it, but had enough money to buy shares in the enterprise. For twenty years thereafter, while other actors' companies quarreled and constantly split up, this company was a band of harmonious, devoted friends. They were also very successful. As a stockholder, Shakespeare received a generous share of the sacks of pennies collected by the gatherers at the theater door; this, in addition to his actor's wages, made him a wealthy man.

Twice in the long Christmas holidays of 1594 the queen commanded the new company to play before her. She paid Shakespeare and two other leading members of the company an additional fee "by way of Her Majesty's reward."

Shakespeare was now thirty years old. Most of the dramatists of any reputation in the previous decade were dead; the brilliant Marlowe had been killed in a tavern brawl by a dagger through his eye. For a while Shakespeare had the field to himself. His output was prodigious. In the first few years of his association with the Chamberlain's Company he wrote *Romeo and Juliet,* full of the most beautiful love poetry in the English language; *The Merchant of Venice;* and *A Midsummer Night's Dream,* bursting with the country images of his boyhood:

> You spotted snakes with double tongue,
> Thorny hedgehogs, be not seen,
> Newts and blindworms, do no wrong,
> Come not near our Fairy Queen.

The Fairy Queen was, of course, Queen Elizabeth to the audience.

Shakespeare was also writing more historical plays, now very different from his early *Henry VI* and *Richard III.* He had come a long way since then. His kings no longer declaimed long-winded speeches full of complicated rhetoric. A famous speech in his new historical play, *Richard II,* used these simple words to tell what was in the hearts of all the Englishmen of the day:

> This royal throne of kings, this sceptered isle . . .
> This fortress built by Nature for herself
> Against infection and the hand of war,
> This happy breed of men, this little world,
> This precious stone set in the silver sea . . .
> This blessed plot, this earth, this realm, this England . . .
> This land of such dear souls, this dear, dear land . . .

Another famous speech with simple, short words was spoken by King Richard, deposed and facing murder:

> For God's sake, let us sit upon the ground
> And tell sad stories of the death of kings:
> How some have been deposed, some slain in war,
> Some haunted by the ghost they have deposed,
> Some poisoned by their wives, some sleeping killed;
> All murdered.

This subject was also in the hearts of Englishmen and of Queen Elizabeth herself. The fact that a monarch might be plotted against, and his crown taken from him, was a constant worry to Renaissance rulers, particularly to Elizabeth, threatened as she was by Mary of Scotland and later the Earl of Essex.

In 1596 the College of Arms granted a coat of arms to the Shakespeare family. Where the unsuccessful merchant, John Shakespeare, had failed, his son, the successful playwright, succeeded. The Shakespeares of Stratford could now call themselves gentlefolk.

To go with this new distinction, Shakespeare bought a large house in Stratford, called New Place, with much land, two barns, and two orchards. The house itself was three-storied, with a gatehouse and servants' quarters and an inner garden courtyard. Later he bought more acres of good farm land. To have a fine country estate and a coat of arms, too, was a triumph for a man who had risked everything to join low-down actors in London some ten years before.

From now on he spent summers in Stratford instead of going on the road with the rest of the company. He worked on his plays and attended to his property, overseeing his garden, bees, doves, and farm animals. In the fall when the city's theatrical season opened again, back he jogged over the bumpy roads to London to be in the thick of things once more. Shakespeare was now so well known that a critic of the day called him "honey-tongued" and "the most excellent among the English" in both comedy and tragedy.

In 1598 Shakespeare's acting company decided to build its own theater in a popular section across the Thames river where the Bear Gardens and two rival theaters were situated. Every day hundreds of Londoners were rowed in little boats by blue-coated wherrymen to this colorful district. Others swarmed over the many-arched London Bridge, covered with tall shops and houses and adorned on its southern end by the heads of traitors bleaching on spikes in the sun.

On this side of the river the Chamberlain's Company built its theater and called it The Globe. It was the most splendid of all the

London Bridge with heads of criminals on spikes in the foreground.

FOLGER SHAKESPEARE LIBRARY, WASHINGTON

playhouses in London and was called "The Glory of the Banke" and "this fair-fitted Globe." In this famous building the finest plays in the English language, if not in the whole world—written by Shakespeare at the peak of his powers—were performed.

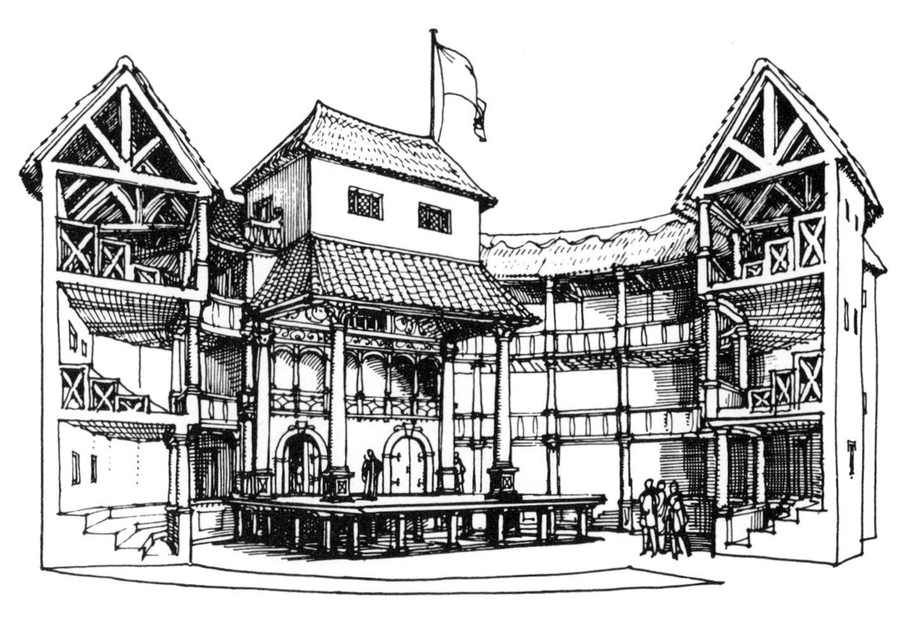

The interior of the Globe may have looked like this.

The Globe Restored BY C. WALTER HODGES

When *Henry V* opened the season in this marvelous new building, its opening chorus apologized for the unworthy stage, this cockpit, this "wooden O." But the audience, from the groundlings whose faces tilted upwards to the sunny stage, to the lords sitting bejeweled in their special balconies, knew that the author did not mean his apology to be taken seriously. The Globe was all that anyone could possibly desire. Its carved woodwork was adorned in the latest fashion with imitation marble, gold and silver, festive tapestries and painted cloths. Banners waved in the wind, and bright ornaments sparkled in the sun. The stage was huge and full of trap doors which promised devils, ghosts, and awesome smoke from the cellar below. A small roof, barely covering half of the stage, had still more trap doors in its brightly decorated, starry underside through which gods, spirits, or huge mechanical birds might descend on ropes. The audience did not feel the need of changing scenery. For them, Shakespeare's great words were enough. When he asked them to imagine the "vasty fields of France" and the mounted knights on the field of Agincourt, it was easy, for Shakespeare's great descriptive language painted the scenery for them.

At the turn of the century Shakespeare was working at a killing pace. New plays were pouring from his pen. They began to take on a different quality. Though all had flashes of his famous humor and many of his equally famous songs, they had parts that were deeply pessimistic and tragic. Maybe this was because so many of the Elizabethan heroes like Essex and Raleigh were toppling from their mighty positions, and the great queen was aging. But certainly Shakespeare was seeing more deeply into all sides of life, both good and bad.

One of the greatest of these new plays was the tragedy of *Hamlet.* Though it had all the popular Renaissance attractions, such as a ghost, duels, poisonings, clowns, conspiracies, a villainous king, and many violent deaths, it had far more. In *Hamlet,* Shakespeare poured out the sorrows of the human heart—unrequited love, hate, disillusion, despair.

In the same years, 1599 and 1600, he managed to produce *Julius Caesar* and two comedies, *As You Like It* and *Twelfth Night.* The latter was played before the queen on Twelfth Night (the end of the Twelve Days of Christmas) in 1601 in the great hall of White-hall palace.

Shakespeare must have been under tremendous pressure most of the time. The creation of these great plays was exhausting, particularly when so much of his time had to be taken up in acting or rehearsing. One of his colleagues later described a man who forced himself to write without rest throughout the night until he fainted from fatigue. We guess that he was describing Shakespeare.

But even on such a dreadful schedule he was always good company. His many friends remarked on his open and free disposition and the gaiety of his conversation. He used to enjoy teasing a devoted friend of his, an up-and-coming playwright called Ben Jonson—and these "wit-combats" at the Mermaid Tavern were compared to the meeting of a great Spanish galleon and an English man-of-war. Jonson was "far higher in Learning; Solid, but Slow in his performances"; Shakespeare, "lesser in bulk but lighter in sailing, could turn with all tides, tack about and take advantage of all winds, by the quickness of his Wit and Invention."

Shakespeare's problems in writing a play were different from a modern dramatist's. Because he had no front curtains, he had to begin a play abruptly with an attention-getting entrance. He had to end the play by an exit of any characters remaining on stage—including the corpses, which had to be carried off somehow as smoothly as possible. There could be no separation of one scene from another except by moving the action rapidly to different parts of the stage, sometimes—although rarely—using an upper balcony for a besieged castle wall, or a small curtained contrivance at the rear for tomb or bed. The whole play had to move swiftly, without stops. Then there was the problem that only boys were used for women's parts. Shakespeare's lovely heroines Juliet and Cleopatra, his villainess Lady Macbeth, his comedienne Juliet's nurse were acted by boys. When their voices changed, they were through.

An enormous amount of work had to be done by the members of the Chamberlain's Company before a play was ready to be performed. It had to be licensed by the official censor. The Globe's scrivener had to copy out separate parts for each actor. There had to be many long rehearsals. Props had to be constructed by the company carpenter—scaling ladders, thrones, coffins, stairs, cages, cauldrons, even enormous birds on which an actor could ride as he was lowered on ropes from trap doors in the overhanging ceiling. Musicians had to practice weird oboe music to be played beneath the stage, or military sounds of drum and trumpet to be sounded from on high, or the music of soft viols and lutes to be played right on stage as an accompaniment to songs and dances.

When all these things had been done, the flag on the topmost gable of the Globe was run up to tell the Londoners on the other side of the river that a play was to be performed that afternoon. The prompter tacked up a big prompt sheet in the corridor behind the stage, with cues and entrances for forgetful actors. The property man got his thrones and chairs in position to be pushed on the big stage when needed.

As the time for the play drew near, the cries of the watermen became louder; the singsongs of the fishwives and orangewives and the man selling "hott pudding-pies hott" pierced the afternoon air; the bears growled in the arena not far away. The crowds began to pour in—army men, gamblers, shops' foremen, apprentices, law students, ladies bringing pillows for their backs, gallants with tobacco pipes and bottles of ale. Even the unemployed came, spending on the play the alms that they should have been spending on their pinched and needy children.

Then suddenly the trumpeter blew a loud call from the roof, and the play was on. The sun gradually sank behind the stage, but the play, without intermissions, did not take long. Before dusk, the cannon boomed at the end of a last stirring scene, and the crowd moved slowly out of the Globe and back across the river to the main part of London.

With busy days like these, the Chamberlain's Company moved from success to success. Shakespeare's fame increased.

In 1603 the Chamberlain's Company was summoned to Richmond Palace to entertain the ailing queen. Her courtiers were sad, for they saw that she was failing daily and had not long to live. Propped up on velvet pillows, sitting very straight, refusing to give in to pain and weakness, Elizabeth watched Shakespeare and the rest of his band of actors for the last time.

The Globe and the Bear Garden on the south bank of the Thames. The main part of London lies on the other side.

FOLGER SHAKESPEARE LIBRARY, WASHINGTON

On March 24, 1603, Queen Elizabeth died. Shakespeare survived her by thirteen years. His debt to her was very great. Because she was a Renaissance queen, with wide interests and a passion for beauty, she had encouraged the growth of the theater, paying no attention to the objections of the Puritans. She knew that great plays would glorify England and her reign. Besides, she enjoyed them. If she had been a different sort of ruler, one who resisted the new currents of Renaissance life, Shakespeare and the other dramatists of that time might have starved in garrets with their plays unwritten.

Fortunately for Shakespeare, the new king, James I, also enjoyed plays and poetry and beautiful language. He heard from everyone that Shakespeare's company was the best in England. Less than two months after Elizabeth's death he took it under his wing. He called it the King's Men, and awarded the actors the honor of wearing the king's livery, giving them each four yards of splendid scarlet cloth.

During the next ten years Shakespeare wrote more than ten plays, and among them were more great tragedies: *Othello, King Lear, Macbeth,* and *Antony and Cleopatra.* We see these plays today with the same emotions that Shakespeare's contemporaries felt. The plays of other Elizabethan dramatists now molder on scholars' shelves, for their stories and characters do not interest the modern theatergoer. But Shakespeare wrote about situations and problems that are as vivid today as in his own time. He wrote about jealousy, ambition, madness, pride, love, grief, and the brevity of life. These tragedies are so tremendous in concept, the characters in them so real and their problems so terrible, and their language so beautiful, that it is hard to imagine one man being able to create them. Yet one of Shakespeare's co-workers wrote that "his mind and hand went together, and what he thought, he uttered with that easiness that we have scarce received from him a blot in his papers."

Perhaps Shakespeare was exhausted by his stupendous creations. In the last years of his life he wrote fewer plays, and no more tragedies. He turned to light comedies, of which the greatest was *The Tempest.* He collaborated on another history play, about Queen Elizabeth's father, Henry VIII. In this he paid a compliment both to Queen Elizabeth and to her successor, King James, for a character in the play prophesies that peace will be achieved in her reign:

> In her days every man shall eat in safety
> Under his own vine, what he plants, and sing
> The merry songs of peace to all his neighbors.

and in James's, great colonies:

> Wherever the bright sun of heaven shall shine
> His honour and the greatness of his name
> Shall be, and make new nations. . . .

During the performance of this play, *Henry VIII,* in early summer of 1613, the Globe Theater had a fatal accident. When the actor who was playing King Henry appeared on the stage, two cannon on the Globe roof were discharged loudly—the usual custom for all royal stage entrances. This time the sound-effects man made a mistake, for out of the mouth of the cannon came a flaming wad which landed on the thatch of the roof above the balconies. At first the audience paid no attention, for its eyes as usual were fixed on Shakespeare's stage, but soon the flame circled the roof. Within an hour the Globe had burned to the ground.

Haunting lines that Shakespeare had written a few years before in *The Tempest* unwittingly provided a fitting epitaph for the famous theater:

> The cloud-capped towers, the gorgeous palaces,
> The solemn temples, the great globe itself,
> Yea, all which it inherit, shall dissolve,
> And, like this insubstantial pageant faded,
> Leave not a rack behind.

Henry VIII was Shakespeare's last play. He stayed in Stratford in the big house that he loved. Friends came up from London to see him, among them two well-loved actor friends who wanted to publish all his work in one volume. Less than half of his plays had been printed during his lifetime, in the form of small pamphlets, called quartos, which sold for sixpence. Some had been secretly sold to printers and were incorrect, badly garbled versions. Now, in 1616, Shakespeare was too tired and ill to bother with editing the hundreds of pages of his plays, scribbled over with stage directions, wrinkled and worn from use by the prompter during countless performances. When he died that April, at the age of fifty-two, his friends knew that their best memorial to him would be to collect and edit the plays they had acted in and loved so well. It took them seven years of "care and paine" before they were able to publish the world's greatest literary masterpiece—the collection of thirty-six plays of William Shakespeare. Called the First Folio, it sold for one pound, a large sum for those days. Three hundred years later someone bought a copy—for one hundred thousand dollars.

The editors wrote an introduction to the Folio, full of affectionate praise for their old friend. His companion and rival playwright, Ben Jonson, added a heartfelt and generous poetical tribute, calling him the star of poets, Sweet Swan of Avon, superior to anything insolent Greece or haughty Rome or any of their successors had produced:

> Soul of the Age!
> The applause! delight! the wonder of our stage!

With Shakespeare's death, the Age of the Renaissance lost its last great soul. Another, sterner age was dawning—the age of scientific achievement, the age of reason rather than passion. The Renaissance, with its galaxy of great rulers, explorers, artists, and writers, had come to an end. During the Renaissance men of the Western World had awakened to their full powers, and in pursuing all that life could offer they achieved one of the most exuberant and creative ages man has known. Its heritage is with us wherever we turn today.

BIBLIOGRAPHY

Books especially recommended for young readers are starred.

Ady, C. M. *Lorenzo dei Medici and the Renaissance.* English Universities Press, Ltd., London, 1955.

Atkinson, W. C. *A History of Spain and Portugal.* Penguin Books, Baltimore, 1960.

*Bargellini, P. *The Medici Palace.* Arnaud, Florence, 1960.

Bartolini, R. *Florence and Its Hills.* W. S. Heinman, New York, 1953.

Black, J. B. *The Reign of Elizabeth, 1559–1603.* Oxford, Clarendon Press, London, 1953.

*Brown, I. *Shakespeare in His Time.* Thomas Nelson and Sons, Edinburgh, 1960.

*Brown, L. A. *Map Making.* Little, Brown and Company, Boston, 1960.

Burkhardt, J. *The Renaissance in Italy.* Harper & Brothers, New York, 1958.

Carrington, C. E. and Jackson, J. H. *History of England.* Cambridge University Press, Cambridge, 1932.

Castiglione, B. *The Courtier.* Anchor Books, Doubleday & Company, Inc., New York, 1959.

Clark, K. *Leonardo Da Vinci.* Penguin Books, Baltimore, 1958.

*Chute, M. *Shakespeare of London.* E. P. Dutton & Co., Inc., New York, 1949.

*——. *Stories from Shakespeare.* The World Publishing Company, Cleveland, 1956.

Columbus, Christopher. *Letter to Luis de Sant' Angel,* facsimile edition. New York Public Library, New York.

Commines, P. de. *Memoirs.* H. G. Bohn, London, 1855.

Dawson, G. E. *Life of William Shakespeare.* Folger Pamphlet, Washington, 1960.

*Debenham, F. *Discovery and Exploration.* Doubleday & Company, Inc., Garden City, 1960.

Dieguez, M. de. *Rabelais par Lui-Meme.* Ecrivains de Toujours, France, 1960.

D'Orliac, F. *Francis the First.* J. B. Lippincott Company, Philadelphia, 1938.

Durant, W. *The Renaissance.* 1953.

——. *The Reformation.* 1957.

——. *The Age of Reason*. 1961.
All Simon and Schuster, Inc., New York.
Doorly, E. *The Story of France*. Jonathan Cape, Ltd., London, 1944.
Elliot, F. *Old Court Life in France*. G. P. Putnam's Sons, New York, 1893.
Gascoigne, G. *Princely Pleasures of Kenilworth*. London.
*Gombrich, E. H. *The Story of Art*. Phaidon Publishers, Inc., Greenwich, Conn., 1953.
Guerard, A. *History of France*. The University of Michigan Press, Ann Arbor, 1959.
——. *Life and Death of an Ideal*. Charles Scribner's Sons, New York, 1928.
Hackett, F. *Francis the First*. Doubleday & Company, Inc., Garden City, N.Y., 1935.
*Hahn, Emily. *Leonardo da Vinci*. Random House, New York, 1956.
*Halliday, F. E. *Shakespeare: A Pictorial Biography*. The Viking Press, Inc., New York, 1957.
Harrison, W. *A Description of the Island of Great Britain*. New Shakespearean Society, London, 1877–8.
Harrison, G. B. *Introducing Shakespeare*. Penguin Books, Baltimore, 1939.
——. *Shakespeare Under Elizabeth*. The University of Michigan Press, Ann Arbor, 1933.
*Hartman, G. *Medieval Days and Ways*. The Macmillan Company, New York, 1953.
Hodges, C. W. *The Globe Restored: A Study of the Elizabethan Theatre*. Coward-McCann, Inc., New York, 1953.
*Horizon. *Book of the Renaissance*. American Heritage Publishing Co., Inc., New York, 1961.
Hotson, L. *Shakespeare's Wooden O*. The Macmillan Company, New York, 1960.
Huisinga, A. H. *Waning of the Middle Ages*. Doubleday & Company, Inc., Garden City, 1954.
Jenkins, E. *Elizabeth the Great*. Coward-McCann, Inc., New York, 1959.
Knight, C. *Popular History of England*. J. Slaughter Co., London.
Laneham, R. *Entertainment at Kenilworth*.
LeFranc, A. *La Vie Cotidienne au Temps de la Renaissance*. Librairie Hachette, Paris, 1938.
Leonardo Da Vinci. *The Notebooks of Leonardo Da Vinci* (ed. by E. MacCurdy). George Braziller, Inc., New York, 1955.
*——. *Selections from the Notebooks of Leonardo Da Vinci* (ed. by I. A. Richter). Oxford University Press, New York, 1952.
Lewis, D. B. W. *Doctor Rabelais*. Sheed and Ward, New York, 1957.
*Life Magazine, ed. *Life's Picture History of Western Man*. Time, Inc., New York, 1951.
Loth, D. *Lorenzo the Magnificent*. New York, 1929.
Machiavelli, N. *The Prince*. Everyman, E. P. Dutton & Co., Inc., New New York, 1951.

Mariejol, J. H. *The Spain of Ferdinand and Isabella*. Rutgers University Press, New Brunswick, 1961.
Mattingly, G. *The Armada*. Houghton Mifflin Company, Boston, 1959.
——. *Catherine of Aragon*. Vintage Books, Alfred G. Knopf, Inc., New York, 1960.
Maurois, A. *A History of France*. Grove Press, New York, 1960.
*Merejkowski, D. *The Romance of Leonardo*. Modern Library, Inc., New York, 1928.
Morison, S. E. *Admiral of the Ocean Sea*. Little, Brown & Co., Boston, 1942.
*——. *Christopher Columbus, Mariner*. Mentor Books, New York, 1946.
Morton, H. V. *A Stranger in Spain*. Dodd, Mead & Co., New York, 1955.
Mumby, F. A. *The Girlhood of Queen Elizabeth*. Houghton Mifflin Company, Boston, 1910.
Neale, J. B. *Queen Elizabeth*. Harcourt, Brace & World, Inc., New York, 1934.
*Neilson, W. A. and Thorndike, A. H. *The Facts About Shakespeare*. The Macmillan Company, New York, 1935.
New Cambridge Modern History. *The Renaissance*, Vol. 1, *The Reformation*, Vol. 3. Cambridge University Press, Cambridge, 1932.
*Nicoll, A. *The Elizabethan*. Cambridge University Press, New York, 1957.
Nichols, J. *Progresses of Queen Elizabeth*.
Nock, A. J. *François Rabelais*. Harper & Brothers, New York, 1929.
——. *A Journey into Rabelais's Country*. William Morrow & Co., Inc., New York, 1934.
Noyes, E. *The Story of Milan*. J. M. Dent, London, 1908.
Parry, J. H. *Europe and a Wider World, 1415–1715*. Hillary House Publishers, Ltd., New York.
Pearson, H. *A Life of Shakespeare*. Walker & Company, New York, 1961.
Pirenne, H. *A History of Europe*, and *Medieval Cities*. Doubleday & Company, Garden City, 1956.
Plattard, J. *Les Oeuvres de Rabelais*. Alfred A. Knopf, Inc., New York, 1910.
Polo, Marco. *Travels of Marco Polo*. The Orion Press, Inc., New York, 1958.
Prescott, W. H. *History of the Reign of Ferdinand and Isabella*. Harper & Brothers, New York, 1845.
Putnam, S. *The Portable Rabelais*. The Viking Press, Inc., New York, 1946.
——. *François Rabelais, Man of the Renaissance*. J. Cape and H. Smith, New York, 1920.
Rabelais, F. *Gargantua and Pantagruel* (translated by Urquhart and Motteux). Encyclopedia Britannica, Inc., Chicago, 1952.
*Richards, D. *Britain Under the Tudors and Stuarts*. Longmans, Green and Co., London, 1958.
*Ripley, E. *Leonardo da Vinci*. Oxford University Press, New York, 1952.
Romier, L. *A History of France* (translated by A. L. Rowse). St. Martin's Press, Inc., New York, 1959.

Ross, J. B. and McLaughlin, M. M., Editors. *Portable Renaissance Reader*. The Viking Press, Inc., New York, 1953.

Reynal & Company, Editors. *Leonardo da Vinci*. Reynal & Company, Inc., New York, 1961.

Rowse, A. L. *The England of Elizabeth*. The Macmillan Company, London, 1951.

——. *The Elizabethans and America*. Harper & Brothers, New York, 1960.

Schevill, F. *The Medici*. Torch Books, Harper & Brothers, New York, 1960.

Shakespeare, W. *Shakespeare's First Folio,* Facsimile Edition. Edited by H. Kokeritz and C. T. Prouty, Yale University Press, New Haven, 1954.

*——. *Folger Library General Reader's Shakespeare*. Edited by L. B. Wright and J. A. Lamar. Pocket Books, Inc., New York.

Shakespeare Survey: An Annual Survey of Shakespearean Study and Production, Vols. 1–13. Cambridge University Press, New York, 1948–1960.

Sichel, E. H. *Women and Men of the French Renaissance*. A. Constable & Co., Westminster, 1901.

Smith, D. N., Editor. *Shakespeare Criticism: A Selection*. Oxford University Press, London, 1916.

Smith, I. *Shakespeare's Globe Playhouse*. Charles Scribner's Sons, New York, 1957.

Tillyard, E. M. W. *Shakespeare's History Plays*. The Macmillan Company, New York, 1947.

Trevelyan, G. M. *History of England*. Doubleday and Company, Inc., Garden City, 1953.

Vallentin, A. *Leonardo da Vinci*. The Viking Press, Inc., New York, 1938.

Van Doren, M. *Shakespeare*. Anchor Books, Doubleday and Company, Inc., Garden City, 1953.

Vasari, G. *Lives of the Artists,* Ed. E. Burroughs, Simon and Schuster, Inc., New York, 1946.

Wescher, H. *Francis I and the Renaissance*. Ciba Review, Basle, 1948.

Wilson, J. D. *The Essential Shakespeare*. Cambridge University Press, Cambridge, 1932.

Wright, L. B. *Shakespeare's Theatre and the Dramatic Tradition*. Folger Booklet, Washington, 1958.

INDEX